I0124082

Helena Rietmann
Ecological Modernization in the United Arab Emirates?

Diskussionspapiere – Wirtschaft, Gesellschaft und Geographie im Vorderen Orient

Herausgegeben von
Steffen Wippel

Band 119

Helena Rietmann

Ecological Modernization in the United Arab Emirates?

The Case of Masdar Eco-City

DE GRUYTER

ISBN 978-3-11-074904-5
e-ISBN (PDF) 978-3-11-074929-8
e-ISBN (EPUB) 978-3-11-074932-8

Library of Congress Control Number: 2021939865

Bibliographic information published by the Deutsche Nationalbibliothek
The Deutsche Nationalbibliothek lists this publication in the Deutsche Nationalbibliografie;
detailed bibliographic data are available on the Internet at http://dnb.dnb.de.

© 2021 Walter de Gruyter GmbH, Berlin/Boston
Printing and binding: CPI books GmbH, Leck

www.degruyter.com

Contents

1   Introduction —— 1

2   Central dimensions of the concept of ecological modernization —— 4
2.1   Three phases of conceptual development —— 4
2.2   Crucial factors in ecological modernization —— 7
2.2.1   Science and technology —— 7
2.2.2   Market dynamics and economic imperatives —— 8
2.2.3   Political and institutional change —— 9
2.2.4   Social movements —— 10
2.2.5   Changing discursive practices and ideology —— 11
2.3   Ecological modernization and cities —— 13

3   Research design —— 15

4   The political-economic context —— 17
4.1   The UAE federal system and power situations —— 17
4.2   The Abu Dhabi roadmap for renewable energy —— 18

5   Ecological modernization in the UAE through the lens of Masdar City —— 22
5.1   Masdar technology —— 22
5.1.1   Renewable energy —— 22
5.1.2   Green building, transportation and carbon capture utilization and storage —— 26
5.2   Economic aspects —— 28
5.2.1   Sovereign wealth funds —— 28
5.2.2   Economic diversification and international trade —— 31
5.3   Institutional framework —— 34
5.3.1   The private departments of sheikh Zayed and his successors —— 34
5.3.2   Governmental institutions —— 35
5.3.3   Public enterprises —— 37
5.4   Environmental groups —— 38
5.4.1   National organizations —— 38
5.4.2   International NGOs and the role of the WWF —— 40

5.5   Environmental education and awareness —— **41**
5.5.1   Educational programs —— **42**
5.5.2   Green Zayedism —— **44**

6   Conclusions —— 46

Literature —— 51

Figures

Fig. 1: Masdar's business units —— 19
Fig. 2: Share of total energy generated in the UAE by Masdar —— 23
Fig. 3: Masdar projects worldwide —— 25
Fig. 4: Share of total energy generated worldwide by Masdar —— 25

Tables

Tab. 1: Synthesis of causal factors in ecological modernization theory —— 13
Tab. 2: Masdar renewable energy projects in the UAE by technology —— 23
Tab. 3: Abu Dhabi sovereign wealth enterprises —— 30
Tab. 4: UAE foreign direct investment (FDI) overview, 2005-2018 —— 32
Tab. 5: Environmental institutional structure in the UAE —— 36
Tab. 6: National and international NGOs with a permanent presence in the UAE —— 40

https://doi.org/10.1515/9783110749298-203

Abbreviations

ADAFSA	Agriculture and Food Safety Authority
ADFD	Abu Dhabi Fund for Development
ADIA	Abu Dhabi Investment Authority
ADIC	Abu Dhabi Investment Council
ADNOC	Abu Dhabi National Oil Company
ADSW	Abu Dhabi Sustainability Week
AI	Artificial intelligence
BREEAM	Building Research Establishment Environmental Assessment Method
CBD	Convention on Biological Diversity
CCUS	Carbon capture utilization and storage
CDM	Clean Development Mechanism
CSP	Concentrating solar power
EAD	Environment Agency Abu Dhabi
EEG	Emirates Environmental Group
EFS	Environment Friends Society
EIP	Eco-industrial park
ERWDA	Environmental Research and Wildlife Development Agency
EU	European Union
EWS	Emirates Nature-WWF (formerly the Emirates Wildlife Society)
FDI	Foreign direct investment
FEA	Federal Environment Agency
FFU	Environmental Policy Research Center
FRT	Freight rapid transit
GCC	Cooperation Council for the Arab States of the Gulf
GONGO	Government-organized non-governmental organization
GRI	Global Reporting Initiative
ICT	Information and communications technology
IMF	International Monetary Fund
IPIC	International Petroleum Investment Company
IRENA	International Renewable Energy Agency
ISO	International Organization for Standardization
ISSP	International Social Survey Program
IUCN	International Union for Conservation of Nature
KU	Khalifa University of Science and Technology
LEED	Leadership in Energy and Environmental Design
MADFEC	Masdar Abu Dhabi Future Energy Company
MI	Masdar Institute

https://doi.org/10.1515/9783110749298-204

MIT	Massachusetts Institute of Technology
MOCCAE	Ministry of Climate Change and Environment
MOEW	Ministry of Environment and Water
NAFTA	North American Free Trade Agreement
NED	National Endowment for Democracy
NGO	Non-governmental organization
OECD	Organization for Economic Co-operation and Development
OHSAS	Occupational Health and Safety Assessment Series
PI	Petroleum Institute
PRT	Personal rapid transit
PV	Solar photovoltaic
QHSSE	Quality, health, safety, security and the environment
SDGs	Sustainable Development Goals
SSC	Species Survival Commission
SWFI	Sovereign Wealth Fund Institute
SWF	Sovereign wealth fund
TAQA	Abu Dhabi National Energy Company PJSC
TEI	Technological environmental innovation
UAE	United Arab Emirates
UK	United Kingdom
UN	United Nations
UNCED	United Nations Conference on Environment and Development
UNEP	United Nations Environment Program
UNFCCC	United Nations Framework Convention on Climate Change
USGBC	United States Green Building Council
WCED	World Commission on Environment and Development
WVS	World Value Survey
WWF	World Wide Fund For Nature

1 Introduction

2018 marked one decade since the beginning of construction work in Masdar City, Abu Dhabi, United Arab Emirates (UAE). Masdar City was introduced as a flagship urban and environmental policy project for the UAE. It was conceived with the intent of fostering sustainable living by designing and constructing a sustainable, low-carbon and zero-waste city (Masdar 2020b). After the UAE's economy had been boosted by commercial oil and gas exploration from the 1960s on, rapid development and growing consumption increased environmental degradation in the country. By 2000, the UAE was ranked second on a global level for its carbon dioxide emissions per capita with a figure of 35.9 metric tons (EU 2019: Annex 5; The World Bank 2020). At the same time, in the early 2000s, sheikh Zayed bin Sultan Al Nahyan (hereafter: Zayed), founding father of the UAE, started to support and enhance environmental state initiatives and projects. In 2008, Masdar City was promoted as the world's first carbon-neutral city (WFES 2008) by sheikh Mohamed bin Zayed, crown prince of Abu Dhabi, putting a strong focus on the innovation and development of renewable energy and further sustainable technologies. The initiation of Masdar City illustrated a new policy strategy of the UAE to promote renewable energy sources and environmental reform (MADFEC 2009).

Theoretically, concepts of "ecological modernization" are used to evaluate environmental reform measures such as increased investment in technological innovation aimed at improving resource efficiency and mitigating environmental degradation. In the context of the UAE, "ecological modernization" as a term has very rarely been used. When it is employed, it is solely as a normative description of a national identification of environmental reform processes that were promoted as "sustainable" and "modern" (Masdar 2016b; WFES 2008). In this analysis I treat ecological modernization as an analytical tool rather than merely a normative description. To that end, I investigate the role of, and the extent to which, the restructuring of production and consumption processes, the establishment of political institutions and the involvement of social groups contribute to a successful implementation of environmental reform. In this paper, I understand "sustainability" as "ecological sustainability", meaning the "ecological conditions necessary to support human life at a specified level of well-being through future generations" (Lélé 1991: 609).

Masdar City is the outcome of an environmental restructuring policy. It is part of the joint venture Masdar, which fosters projects on renewable energy and sustainability, water and waste management, sustainable agriculture and energy and material efficiency. In mainstream literature and the public discourse, Masdar City has been branded a "smart" city. "Smart" cities are mainly based on

https://doi.org/10.1515/9783110749298-001

information and communication technologies that aim to enhance economic growth and provide an improved social, physical and economic infrastructure (Albino et al. 2015: 4).

My analysis examines the process of ecological modernization in the UAE as observed in the case of Masdar City.[1] The analysis will be guided by the following question: What factors explain ecological modernization in the UAE within the context of Masdar City? More precisely, I analyze how the factors of (1) technological innovation, (2) economic dynamics, (3) political institutional change, (4) social actors and (5) changing discursive practices and ideology affect the development of Masdar City and to what extent they are helpful in analyzing ecological modernization the UAE. I apply a theoretical body of political science literature on ecological modernization to assess these changes. In addition, my paper will refer to and include several theoretical aspects from the fields of human ecology, regional and global studies, and urban research. These reference points embed the topic within debates of "modernity", regional studies on the Arab countries of the Persian Gulf, and sustainable urbanity.

A lot of work on Masdar City has been done from a technical and natural sciences perspective, mostly concentrating on the UAE's approaches in the field of renewable energy (Al-Amir/Abu-Hijleh 2013; Almheiri 2015; Doukas et al. 2006; Foreman 2007; Hindley 2007; Jones 2008; Madichie 2011). Moreover, Masdar City has been an object of research in the discipline of urban studies, which evaluates the project in terms of sustainable building, architecture, and urbanism (Crot 2013; Cugurullo 2013a, 2013b, 2016a, 2016b; Günel 2019; Brorman Jensen 2014; Texier/Doulet 2016; Theys 2011; Woessner 2016). Moreover, I find very few contributions that elaborate on ecological modernization and the UAE. Reiche (2010a, 2010b) tackles ecological modernization by studying "environmental improvements" (Reiche 2010a: 2397), while Al-Saidi and Elagib (2018) understand ecological modernization as a normative approval of environmental reform in the UAE. Furthermore, Al-Saidi et al. (2019), Luciani (2016), Luomi (2009, 2014) and Raouf (2008) question environmental policy shifts of the UAE within international climate negotiations in the regional context of the Cooperation Council for the Arab States of the Gulf (GCC). Both her dissertation project as well as later contributions of Ouis (2002a, 2002b, 2010) constitute important works in the context of tradition, modernity and environment in the UAE. Ouis (2011) embeds modernization in societal traditions of the UAE and considers the public discourse on environmental reform and modernization.

---

1 This paper is a compacted and revised version of my master thesis, submitted in 2020 at the Otto Suhr Institute of Freie Universität Berlin.

My work is a contribution to the theoretical body and paradigm of ecological modernization. It adds to the geographic coverage of this concept in countries of the Global South, in my case, the Arab countries of the Persian Gulf. The study aims to operationalize the concept of ecological modernization for an analytical framework containing five "factors" which characterize and help to investigate ecological modernization. Furthermore, I transfer the concept of ecological modernization from the field of *national* environmental politics and transformation to the scale of *urban* structures, particularly to "smart" or "sustainable" cities. Masdar City has effectively been promoted by the UAE government as a "global leader" in renewable energy. Therefore, in a broader context, my paper aims to shed light on the arguable self-image of the UAE leadership regarding international climate ambitions. In my subsequent analysis, I strongly distance my following assumptions from the usage of the term "modernity" in its one-sided dimension that reproduces a hierarchical power relation between countries in the Global North and the Global South.

This paper proceeds as follows. Chapter 2 focuses on the theoretical foundations of ecological modernization. I will describe three phases of conceptual development, in which I identify central topics developed by the protagonists of ecological modernization. These topics include science and technology, ecology and economy and political modernization. In a second step, I incorporate these "topics" into the above-mentioned five "factors". They constitute the analytical framework for the following empirical study to investigate what role these factors play and to what extent they contribute to the alleged development of ecological modernization in the UAE. This chapter also connects ecological modernization and urban structures. Chapter 3 covers the research method in terms of approach, data collection and limitations of my research. Chapter 4 situates the study in the political-economic context of the UAE and gives an overview of the origins of Masdar City. Chapter 5 presents the empirical findings and the impact of the previously elaborated factors on ecological modernization in the UAE. The paper concludes with Chapter 6, which summarizes and synthesizes the results from the empirical analysis and places them in a theoretical perspective.

2 Central dimensions of the concept of ecological modernization

2.1 Three phases of conceptual development

The concept of ecological modernization arose in the beginning of the 1980s, when environmental change became a political topic, which occurred mostly in societies of the Global North (Hajer 1995: 73). In that context, the "Our Common Future" report (also known as the Brundtland report) published by the World Commission on Environment and Development (WCED) in 1987 and the World Summit on Environment and Development in Rio de Janeiro in 1992 raised environmental concerns such as biological diversity loss, climate change, desertification and water scarcity as "global phenomena" (Mol et al. 2009: 5). This led to the introduction of the notion of "sustainable development" and catalyzed the debate on the divergent priorities of economic development and environmental protection.[2]

With his speech at the Berlin House of Representatives, the Parliament of the state of Berlin, in 1982, scholar Martin Jänicke claimed to have coined the phrase "ecological modernization": in his speech as deputy, he proposed to the government to introduce an environmental policy for the processing, energy, transport, and construction sectors. In Jänicke's conception, this policy should implement the development of technological innovation and streamline energy and raw material consumption; hence, it should push forward the "ecological modernization" in these four sectors (Abgeordnetenhaus von Berlin 1982: 789f). Jänicke's case had two implications for the concept of ecological modernization: First, ecological modernization has emerged as a normative political notion. In this understanding, ecological modernization refers to a state's policy strategy to prescribe "environmental reform processes at multiple scales in the contemporary world" (Mol et al. 2009: 4). Second, ecological modernization has evolved as a theoretical analytical concept: According to Mol et al. (ibid.), the concept of ecological modernization refers to the "scientific interpretation of environmental reform", that is, a growing body of scholarship and studies that reflect on how "[...] various institutions and social actors attempt to integrate environmental concerns into their everyday functioning, development and relationships with others, including their relation with the natural world".

---

2 For a comprehensive discussion of the term "sustainable development", the Club of Rome's "Limits to Growth" (1972) and "Blueprint for Survival" (Goldsmith/Allen 1972) are to be included.

https://doi.org/10.1515/9783110749298-002

In addition to Jänicke, sociologist and human ecologist Joseph Huber (1983, 1985) shaped early academic work on the concept of ecological modernization. For him, modern environmental problems do not have their roots solely in technological concerns, but emerge from their socio-economic context (Huber 1983: 1). Hence, an "environmental problem" or the "ecological question" (ibid.: 4f) reflects both technical and political-economic dependencies, and the conflict between the industrial system and the natural environment. In this context, any "environmental policy as a process of modernization" (Huber 1993: 51)[3] was considered a contradiction in itself until the mid-1980s, as modernization had been "essentially about industrialization and economic growth[4] and these were considered to be the main causes of environmental problems" (ibid.). However, in the beginning of the 1980s, a perspective of "ecological growth" emerged in which ecology and economy were not considered as opponents, but both benefited from investments in labor-saving technologies and innovations (ibid.: 56).

Between the late 1980s and the mid-1990s, ecological modernization focused on technological innovation in industrial production (Jänicke 1993: 18). According to Hartje (1990: 137), the traditional debate on technology in environmental reforms seemed obsolete. It was "tackled head on" (ibid.): technological progress had to be accelerated. Consequently, technical measures were proposed, which aimed at preventing air, water and soil pollution and increasing material and energy efficiency. For Huber (1993: 60), ecological modernization is the "gradual or continuous rationalization of the behavior of environmentally relevant actor groups, in particular industry and commerce, consumers, voters, media, science, politics, government and public authorities". The process of ecological rationalization is carried out on multiple levels of action, which systematically condition each other. Furthermore, the development of legal bases for political action and decision-making should ensure rational administrative procedures and a change in the socio-cultural rationality of actions or norms through the change of attitudes, changed value priorities, and preferences. According to Huber (2004: 22), one of the basic aims behind the concept of ecological modernization is "to conceive a way of environmental problem solving on the basis of science and technology, which would not fundamentally oppose industrialization". Instead,

---

3 Unless otherwise indicated, translations are mine.
4 "Economic growth" here refers to the one-sided quantitative interpretation of "continued population growth in connection with urbanization, [..] the continued increase in production due to mass consumption and economies of scale [and ..] the wear and tear of raw materials, energy and fossil resources" (Huber 1993: 52).

processes of industrial development and modernization should be readapted to the "state-of-the-art technology" (ibid.) with respect to ecological considerations.

Since the beginning of the 1990s, the notion of ecological modernization began to consider the institutional and cultural dynamics of industrial production in advanced industrialized nations, both on the national and, comparatively, on the transnational level. In this context, ecological modernization emerged as a social theory. As Buttel (2009: 130) explains, this concept of ecological modernization deals with the changing role of the state within state-society relations. More precisely, the central idea is to transform "the institutions of modernity to such an extent that they can meet the requirements of a necessary ecological restructuring of society" (Mol 1995: 25). According to this view, processes of ecological modernization require certain state structures, policy networks and policy cultures (Mol/Spaargaren 1992: 324).

During the 2000s, the concept of ecological modernization broadened its theoretical and geographical scope. Because ecological modernization had exclusively been regarded in countries in the Global North, it was criticized for following a "eurocentric" approach to state policies (Choy 2007: 14). According to Mol (2000: 92), this "eurocentrism" was based in the socio-political, economic as well as cultural conditions and institutions that characterized the geographical scope where both researchers and their objects of study were located. Yet, since the mid-1990s, studies on ecological modernization have expanded into Central and Eastern Europe and into the Global South, mainly to countries in South-East Asia. Frijns et al. (2000: 258), for instance, identified key institutional characteristics required for ecological restructuring in West-European countries and applied them to the case of Vietnam. These factors include a democratic and open political system, a legitimate and interventionist state with socio-environmental institutional capacities, the existence of a civil society, business organizations, tradition in negotiating and policy-making, a detailed system of environmental monitoring, state-regulated market economy that underlies production and consumption processes, and advanced technological development.

Furthermore, Frijns et al. (ibid.: 259) explain that in a "globalizing world, with modern industrialized countries still providing the dominant models of 'economic' development, models of ecological reform that are believed to be inappropriate for non-OECD countries at first sight, might still be 'imposed' [...] upon these countries through a diversity of mechanisms". In this context, development programs imposed by Global North countries and international actors, such as the World Bank or the International Monetary Fund (IMF), the declarations of the United Nations Conference on Environment and Development (UNCED) as well as the United Nations Framework Convention on Climate Change (UNFCCC), facilitate the transfer of environmental technology from the Global North to the Global South. As a consequence, ecological modernization scholars tend to consider processes of environmental reform in the Global South only through the perspective of the "westernization" of environmental reform, occurring through environmental negotiations, financial and technical assistance, the scientific-technological exchange of ideas and experiences, global firms and international environmental non-governmental organizations (NGOs) (ibid.).

2.2 Crucial factors in ecological modernization

Mol and Sonnenfeld (2000) provided an early framework for investigating the processes of ecological modernization. Their work describes a number of factors, such as science and technology, market dynamics and economic imperatives, political and institutional change, social movements, and changing discursive practices and ideology which affect these processes.

2.2.1 Science and technology

According to the analytical concept of ecological modernization, science and technology present a core aspect in the socio-ecological transformation process. As Mol and Sonnenfeld (2000: 6) explain, science and technology cause environmental problems, but simultaneously are valued for their "actual and potential role in curing and preventing them". Among ecological modernization scholars, Huber (1995, 2004) has provided the theoretical groundings for understanding technological innovations. Hence, environmental problem solving needs to be technological as "environmental problems are perturbations of ecological systems of which humankind is part by way of physical operations carried out through its instrumental capacities" (Huber 2004: 7). Following the concept of ecological modernization, environmental problem solving does not entirely oppose industrialization on account of science and technology (ibid.: 22). Yet, processes of industrial development and modernization are to be ecologically readapted, by inventing and designing state-of-the-art technologies.

Huber (ibid.: 3) introduces the term technological environmental innovations (TEIs). This category is not limited to environmental technologies like exhaust-air catalytic converters, filters in chimneys or sewage water purification plants, which all belong to environmental downstream measures that rely on "end-of-pipe" technologies (so called "add-on" measures in environmental state activity). Downstream measures refer to technologies that are used when damage or pollution have already occurred and do not induce an upstream change of the environmental problem. Furthermore, TEIs have not only been developed for environmental reasons, but represent a "new generation of innovative technologies" describing upstream measures which fulfill both ecological criteria and technical criteria such as efficiency, operational safety and reliability (ibid.). Rather, TEIs are designed for cleaner and better industrial processes aiming to establish new structures and innovations instead of increasing the productivity of old and suboptimal structures. According to Huber (ibid.: 5), new technologies therefore tend to have a "much bigger learning curve potential" than old technologies which are inflexible, rigid and may even cause the reproduction of environmental perturbation. However, TEIs are only implemented when they match price and profitability of conventional technologies (ibid.: 7).

2.2.2 Market dynamics and economic imperatives

According to Mol (1997: 141), the concept of ecological modernization focuses on the importance of economic and market dynamics in ecological reform and the changing relation between the state and the market. Mol (1997) and Mol and Sonnenfeld (2000) explain that entrepreneurs, innovators and other "economic agents" (ibid.: 6) such as producers, customers, consumers, credit institutions and insurance companies should act as "social carriers" (Mol 1997: 141) of ecological restructuring. More precisely, economic push and pull factors, which lead to new political arrangements between private and public actors as well as to the assignment of traditional state competencies in environmental protection to market institutions, are presumed to cause environmental reform and transformation (Mol 2000: 51). The concept of ecological modernization assumes that the market economy is the "most effective way of securing the flexibility, innovation and responsiveness needed to promote the ecological adaptation of industry" (Blowers 1997: 853). Thus, industries are actively included in the ecological transformation process, constituting a "progenitor [...] of the global economy and [...] regarded as the initiators of change" (ibid.).

Furthermore, embedding ecological modernization in the context of globalization, Mol (2002: 95) states that globalization of the world economy has caused environmental problems. In this regard, globalization has often been associated with the dynamics of global capitalism which represent the "root" of environmental destruction. Notwithstanding, certain economic mechanisms and dynamics redirect global capitalist developments by triggering or mediating environmental reform, provided that they are put under pressure by the state, civil society and citizen-consumer demand (ibid.: 102f). Transnational industrial companies, global markets and trade, global information and communication networks and companies and global and regional institutions[5] are playing an active role in this dynamism. Following Mol (2001: 97), companies may impose their requirements on their suppliers in the form of environmental management systems, new environmental technologies, cleaner production methods and new organizational principles that include environmental issues. However, even if market dynamics present a driver for economy-mediated environmental innovations and transformations, they are far from "sufficient" (Mol 2002: 103). Capitalist economic mechanisms and institutional arrangements will always prioritize economic logics and rationalities, which often do not conform with environmental reform. Therefore, against neoliberal assumptions of leaving environmental decisions to the market and economic institutional arrangements, effective environmental policy requires environmental institutions at the state level and an environmental movement in the civil society (ibid.: 104). In addition, Choy (2007: 18) views the implementation of environmental certification and the eco-labeling of products as relevant in ecological modernization. According to him, "supply chain pressure" (ibid.: 19) broadens the market access for companies and helps to achieve competitive advantage in the global market. For Mol (1997: 141), this articulation of environmental "standards" anticipates the "economiz[ation of] ecology", leading to the harmonization of national environmental practices, regimes and standards (Mol 2001: 96) and enhances initiatives for environmentally friendly products and processes in industrial sectors (Choy 2007: 19).

2.2.3 Political and institutional change

Traditionally, the "welfare state" (Mol 2000: 51) implements "command-and-control" strategies in a hierarchical, centralized, and reactive manner to solve environmental degradation problems (Choy 2007: 17). However, scholars have found that these strategies were not sufficiently effective in the prevention of environmental degradation. Consequently, policymakers started collaborating with private or market institutions in environmental state directives. Jänicke (1993: 25) depicts the changing relationship between the state and the market for the concept of ecological modernization as the process of "political modernization".

---

5 These include regional organizations such as the European Union, multilateral treaties such as the North American Free Trade Agreement (NAFTA) and international financial institutions such as the World Bank.

According to him, this change should not only touch upon technological innovation (the "ongoing modernization"). Instead, he expects a transformational process which comes with a "renewal" of institutional arrangements and paradigm shifts, portraying the "engine of long-term development spurts" (ibid.: 16). Political modernization hence presumes the institutionalization and differentiation of a new technological, political-social and scientific-cultural problem solution arrangement (ibid.: 17), in which participative structures and the openness of the decision-making mechanisms are considered as important prerequisites for environmental success (Jänicke 1996: 22). However, participative structures are deemed to require an "integrative capacity" of the political system, that is the "openness of input mechanisms" and the integrative implementation of innovative approaches (ibid., quoted from Kitschelt 1983). In other terms, he demands the ability to achieve consensus and integration.

In this context, Jörgens (1996: 62ff; 73) describes the institutionalization of environmental reform thus: An environmental ministry prepares and implements environmental law and environmental programs and determines environmental standards. It has a representative function on the international level and promotes research and consultancy. Moreover, an environmental office (agency) might observe and evaluate the environmental situation and policy. Yet, it might also have certain executive competencies in environmental policy. Furthermore, a committee of environmental experts advises the ministry and the environmental office and assigns contracts to research institutions. An independent environmental report helps to inform the public. Governments also implement an environmental framework law, which usually includes the programmatic design and formulation of environmental principles and goals. As soon as governments include environmental norms in constitutional law, environmental protection measures become legally binding and strengthened against other policy areas. Mol and Sonnenfeld (2000: 7) highlight the importance of supranational institutions for the nation state's role in environmental reform. According to them, environmental conferences are to determine political arrangements in environmental state behavior.

2.2.4 Social movements

According to Mol (2000: 51), the transformation of the state-market relationship has forced environmental organizations to reconsider their "attitude and strategy towards both domains and to invent new ways of making use of these transformations in pushing for environmental reform". Therefore, the state, represented by its environmental organizations and institutions, is no longer expected to be a "natural ally" (ibid.) of the environmental movement. Social movements have increasingly been involved in public as well as private decision-making institutions in environmental reforms (Mol/Sonnenfeld 2000: 7). More precisely, the sphere of influence of environmental organizations has no longer been, unlike their position in the 1970s and 1980s, limited to the outside observer of governmental processes and institutions, but they have succeeded to act both as a "watchdog" and/or a partner in decision-making (ibid.: 8).

Mol (2000: 47) underlines three core processes that have affected social movements, namely the changing ideology that predominates in the environmental movement, modifications in the position of environmental organizations against other actors and transformations in the strategic operations of such organizations between the state and the market. First, the traditional opposition of environmental organizations in the 1970s against capitalist production, complex technologies, industrialization and state bureaucracies as the roots of environmental harm, was replaced by an increased recognition for technological innovation as a solution to the ecological crisis (ibid.: 48). Second, considering themselves as part of a broader movement, environmentalists of the 1970s were engaging in solidarity and common political agendas with other movements struggling for social change in societies of the Global North, such as the peace movement or anti-nuclear organizations. In the 1990s, however, environmental movements oriented their political agenda towards the reformation and the "fine tuning" (ibid.) of existing environmental institutions. To achieve environmental goals, the movement decoupled the ecological agenda from those political aims constituting other social perspectives and ideologies, such as socialism, conservatism and liberalism. Third, as state and market arrangements began to break the previous barriers between them, environmental groups were increasingly involved in the dynamic process of coalition building between the state, the market and social groups, to maximize and safeguard environmental gains (ibid.: 49).

2.2.5 Changing discursive practices and ideology

Furthermore, Mol and Sonnenfeld (2000: 7) emphasize changing discursive practices and new ideologies as another relevant factor for ecological modernization. According to them, the confrontation of economic and environmental interests should not be accepted as a legitimate position. Mol and Spaargaren (1992: 329) identify three schools of thought in relation to modernity and the environmental crisis. First, following Schnaiberg's "treadmill of production" theory (1980), neo-

Marxist scholars state that a small number of powerful organizations continuously drive the process of capital accumulation (ibid.: 209). In this context, the ecological crisis is strongly linked to the capitalist character of modern society. Theorists of the counterproductivity persuasion are aligned with the environmental movement on this matter. According to this view, Marxist theory undertheorizes the forces of production, that is the hierarchical character of the industrial production that harms nature (Mol/Spaargaren 1992: 330). Hence, the "myth of the great machine" (ibid.), the organization of the industrial system, is linked to counter consequences of the goals it was designed for. These include the increasing discrepancy of welfare in terms of a growing gross domestic product against the well-being of humankind and nature. Post-industrial society theorists, on the contrary, assume that "the development of industry and its impact on society [were] the central features of modern states" (Badham 1984: 2). More precisely, "social thought [...] becomes concerned with the social requirements of industrial development, the social structures that either facilitate or hinder the efficient pursuit of industry, and the impact of industrial development upon society" (ibid.).

Mol and Spaargaren (1992: 336), however, state that ecological modernizing presumes to overcome the traditional debate on capitalist production. As Huber (1985: 77f) emphasizes, capitalism is not considered as relevant in overcoming the ecological problem. According to him (ibid.), "capitalism is nothing indecent, but a given quality of our age". Ecological modernization focuses on technologically induced developments within the industrial system (Mol/Spaargaren 1992: 336). The ecological "switchover" is expected to be the "logical, necessary and inevitable next stage" in the development of the industrial system, so that the system is able to correct its construction fault of impacting the environment by itself (ibid.). For Huber (1989: 10f), ecological modernization thus concentrates on the relationship between a technocratic system (rather than the industrial system, see Mol/Spaargaren 1992: 337) and the environment while emphasizing the effect of production in the industrial system on the depletion of natural resources and the pollution of the environment in relation to the sustenance base. Cohen (2000: 78) raises a socio-cultural dimension of the concept of ecological modernization. According to him, ecological knowledge and information enhance the citizens' "ecological consciousness", which is the outcome of values, emotions and the quest for "good life" of the individual's judgment of the environment (ibid.: 81). More precisely, environmental knowledge is to transform into an ideology that people can "appropriate (or reject) to define their personal identities" (ibid.). Hence, by using environmental knowledge, based on scientific outputs, in the public discourse, people send social signals to one another as by means of "wearing a certain article of clothing" (ibid.).

Tab. 1: Synthesis of causal factors in ecological modernization theory
Source: Own illustration.

	Factor	Operationalization
1	Science and technology	Science and research Innovative technologies
2	Market dynamics and economic imperatives	Economic agents International trade
3	Political and institutional change	Public-private arrangements Institutionalization
4	Social groups	Environmental movements
5	Changing discursive practices and ideology	Ecology and economy Ecological consciousness

2.3 Ecological modernization and cities

Few contributions connect ecological modernization and cities. According to Davoudi et al. (2009: 15) who focus on climate change and urban planning by considering politics, values, governance, legislation and institutional capacity, urbanity is a basic component of governance and a key factor for the government's capacity to respond effectively to climate change and other challenges related to sustainable development. Owens (1994: 446) highlights that the issue of sustainable development has early been applied to political decision-making for cities, compared to other policy fields. At the same time, political decisions, fiscal policy, and private investments have curbed cities' targets to reduce emissions (Davoudi et al. 2009: 15). These include for example the "taboo" of increasing fuel taxes and low levels of investment in public transport and renewable energy (ibid.). Moreover, Antrobus (2011: 207) regards cities within the "pragmatic scale of governance" in respect to the ecological crisis. Therefore, cities present a new form of "hope" to reduce the effects of an ecological disaster, in which "civic leaders have been dreaming green dreams" (ibid.). City administrations thus are expected to "desire to be 'the greenest city'" (ibid.) by installing photovoltaic cells on homes, building windmills and producing energy by hydroelectric turbines, and expecting green jobs based on technology and innovation. However, cities should also implement specific low-carbon actions to improve resiliency.

For the last two decades, debates about the future of urban development have increasingly been influenced by the discussion about "smart cities" (Hollands 2008: 303). Having mostly started in countries of the Global North,

Hollands (2008: 304) quotes from the 1997 World Forum on Smart Cities which suggested that around 50,000 cities and towns worldwide develop smart initiatives over the next decade. Hence, cities around the world have started to introduce solutions which enable transportation linkages, mixed land use and high-quality urban services with both economic and environmental benefits in the long run (Albino et al. 2015: 4). Many of these urban services are based on information and communication technologies (ICTs) which help to create what is named in academia, urban planning, politics and business as "smart city". Yet, the term "smart city" reflects just one of the latest developments in urban planning and socio-demographic terminology in a row of new city categories which have entered the policy discourse. De Jong et al. (2015: 26) explain that in most cases, "smart" was supplemented by further categories to describe urban-based technological change and implementations of e-governance (i.e., the "digital city", "intelligent city" or "information city"), the relation of information technology, knowledge and culturally creative industries (namely the "knowledge city" and "creative city"; Hollands 2008: 304) and the enhancement of social and environmental sustainability ("sustainable city", "resilient city", "eco-city", "low carbon city", as well as combinations of these: "low carbon eco-city" and "ubiquitous eco-city").

However, as Hollands (2008: 304) states, there have been very few analyses of the smart city discourse taking a critical perspective. According to him, especially ideas which follow the "entrepreneurial city" model (Harvey 1989: 3), in which neoliberal policies and competition dominate and shape macroeconomic outcomes, are rarely questioned. In this context, van Koppen and Mol (2009: 312f) highlight two elements which may provide connecting points for the concept of ecological modernization for eco-cities. Eco-cities can serve as focal points for networks of regional and international companies and provide platforms for knowledge exchange and collective innovation. Furthermore, these networks may promote the creation of regional niches for environmental innovation. For the upcoming analysis, I will concentrate on Masdar City in a "sustainable" as well as "eco-city" interpretation.

3 Research design

My work embraces a qualitative case study approach, that is, the "intensive study of a single unit for the purpose of understanding a larger class of (similar) units" (Gerring 2004: 342). In other terms, the specification of a theoretical framework and the detailed study of one case, namely Masdar City, allows me to gain both inductive and deductive insights into higher-order interactions, here on the emirate and federal realms (Bennett/Elman 2006: 467). However, the choice for a research design with a single case unit has clear limitations. Primarily, my work aims to situate what factors explain ecological modernization processes in a country. Furthermore, my analysis will provide information on the correlative or proximate causal relationship between aspects of ecological modernization in Masdar City and the relevance of the concept for the entire UAE. For the qualitative study of authoritarian regimes, like the UAE,[6] the central challenge is the choice of questions and answers researchers develop when data seem relatively fabricated and trivial (Art 2016: 974f). In this context, scholars often lack the type of data that would allow them to "test causal mechanisms that rely on institutional dynamics, elite attitudes, or other phenomena that are not readily observable" (ibid.: 978).

This paper is based on the study of primary and secondary sources. On the domestic level, I primarily collected empirical material from governmental sources both on a federal (UAE) and emirate (Abu Dhabi) level regarding the environmental policy planning and implementation process. Specifically, I included material from the UAE Ministry of Climate Change and Environment (MOCCAE), the Federal Environment Agency (FEA) and the Abu Dhabi-based Environment Agency (EAD). In addition, I analyzed UAE and Abu Dhabi law on environmental issues as well as environmental state reports. Moreover, I relied on private material from the UAE leader sheikh Zayed and his successors, which plays an important role in the national discourse on nature and environment, as published by their corresponding private departments. Furthermore, I extracted data from official material of the Masdar Abu Dhabi Future Energy Company (MADFEC). These publications and other promotional material proved relevant in comparing Masdar's promotion by officials to the international scholarly perception of Masdar City. Domestic newspapers, written or translated into English,

---

6 According to Freedom House (2020), the UAE is categorized as "not free" based on indicators targeting political rights and civil liberties. It operates on the assumption that freedom is best achieved in liberal democratic societies.

https://doi.org/10.1515/9783110749298-003

which I accessed from their websites, provided an important source of information to trace policy implementation paths in several environmental reform projects conducted by or linked to Masdar. Only few non-governmental organizations or other actors are active in the field of environmental topics. However, I considered material from the World Wide Fund For Nature (WWF) as relevant. Informational material from the International Renewable Energy Agency (IRENA) also provided me with data on the state of the art of renewable energy in the UAE.

As this project touches on social, economic, political, technical and environmental changes, it has been necessary to rely to a great extent on secondary sources and relevant studies from researchers and scholars in English, French and German. Most material published by governmental authorities in the UAE, be it policy documents, reports or other material, as well as newspapers and publications from organizations, is published both in English and in Arabic. Furthermore, previous field work conducted by Luomi (2009, 2014), Ouis (2002a, 2002b, 2010) as well as Reiche (2010a, 2010b) provided additional material for certain aspects of the analysis.

Masdar City has been under construction for a period of fourteen years from 2007 until the present. My work covers the complete project period. Between 2009 and 2012, the global financial crisis and the ambition of project goals affected the scale of Masdar City (Mascarenhas 2018: 70). Within the period from 2012 to the present, Masdar City has developed in its scope, research ambitions, technological focus, institutional building and in collaboration with private partners (Masdar 2018b). Masdar City has been the frontrunning project of the UAE environmental reforms, incorporating renewable energy technologies, urban sustainability and green building, research and science and collaboration with private actors both on a domestic and international level. Policy-decisions made and implemented on the level of Masdar City seem closely linked to environmental policy on the emirate level of Abu Dhabi and the federal level of the UAE. Therefore, Masdar City provides considerable insight into the course of ecological reform through the lens of ecological modernization for the UAE.

4 The political-economic context

4.1 The UAE federal system and power situations

This chapter embeds Masdar City in the political-economic context of federal UAE polity. Masdar City was initiated in the context of an economic roadmap for the emirate of Abu Dhabi. The UAE is a federation of the seven emirates Abu Dhabi (where the capital is located), Ajman, Dubai, Fujairah, Ras Al-Khaimah, Sharjah and Umm Al-Quwain. On the federal level, the UAE is responsible for the issues of foreign affairs, defense and security, medical and educational services, and citizenship and immigration (The Constitution of the UAE[7]: Article 120). Since the foundation in 1971, there has been a power sharing agreement between the emirates of Abu Dhabi and Dubai. The ruler of Abu Dhabi is the president of the UAE, whereas the ruler of Dubai is the prime minister. The rulers of all seven emirates are members of the Supreme Council (the executive authority), though only the rulers of Abu Dhabi and Dubai have a veto mandate (ibid.: Article 49; Taryam 1987: 203). The jurisdiction of environmental policy lies with the individual emirates' governments. Moreover, according to the constitution, "natural resources and wealth in each emirate shall be considered the public property of that emirate" (The Constitution of the UAE: Article 23). Therefore, each oil-producing emirate (Abu Dhabi, Dubai and Sharjah) has the exclusive control over its resources. Moreover, as the Abu Dhabi territory contains the highest concentration of oil and natural gas reserves with 94 percent of the total UAE reserves in 2017 (Dargin 2010: 1; EIA 2017: 3), Abu Dhabi is the wealthiest emirate and represents the financial mainstay of the federation (Heard-Bey 1982: 389). As Reiche (2010b: 379) states, this illustrates one of the main explanations for its regional and global public recognition, especially as major domestic issues are regulated on the emirate level rather than the federal level.

Each of the seven emirates has its own ruler who holds his position because he is the senior personality in one of the leading families of the respective emirate and is likely to be succeeded by his eldest son or brother (Rugh 1997: 18). Moreover, the UAE does not present a historical or geographical entity, but needs to be

---

7 At the time of its establishment in December 1971, the UAE set a written, provisional, and rigid constitution, representing a document agreed upon by all emirates. This constitution was "provisional" because it commonly provided a mechanism for postponing final decisions. A "rigid" or "flexible" constitution refers to the extent to which the provisions could or could not be amended quickly (Taryam 1987: 199). In 1996, the UAE's federal Supreme Council made the provisional constitution permanent.

https://doi.org/10.1515/9783110749298-004

defined in terms of families and their traditional territories (Ouis 2002b: 54). These entities, however, were characterized by changing economic situations and political alliances (ibid.: 55). The rulers of Abu Dhabi descend and succeed from the Al Nahyan family (who belong to the Al Bu Falah group of families), whereas the Dubai emirate is governed by the Al Maktoum (who are part of the Al Bu Falasah families) (ibid.: 57). Thereby, UAE politics have largely been dependent on the quality of its leader(s). Koury (1980: 6) explains that (1) a leader's circumstances, that is the specific situation of the rulership, (2) characteristics of the individual who assumes leadership and (3) the interaction between leader and followers affect his leadership qualities. In my study, personal variables of founding father of the UAE, sheikh Zayed bin Sultan Al Nahyan, such as family background, and socioeconomic situation will be relevant for the analysis of ecological modernization. Furthermore, the UAE political system does not show any of the attributes of a democracy such as regular elections for public office, strong non-governmental "civil society" institutions or a middle class wholly independent of the government (Rugh 1997: 18). Although the first elections were held in the UAE in 2006, half of the members of the legislature, the Federal National Council, are still appointed by the rulers (Reiche 2010b: 379). In every emirate government, both the executive and the consultative council are to a large extent selected by the ruler and only a few members gained their positions through votes.

4.2 The Abu Dhabi roadmap for renewable energy

In 2006, sheikh Mohamed bin Zayed Al Nahyan, crown prince of Abu Dhabi and chairman of the Executive Council, announced that the Abu Dhabi Council for Economic Development and the Department of Planning and Economy would develop a long-term economic vision. The vision aimed to align all economic policies and plans in one common framework and involve the private sector in its implementation (The Government of Abu Dhabi 2008: 1). Its objective was to identify the key enablers for economic growth and to define an economic policy outlook for the emirate through the year 2030. Based on the foundations set by the Abu Dhabi Policy Agenda 2007/08, the roadmap was designed to achieve a "safe and secure society and a dynamic, open economy" (ibid.: 6). This agenda presented a public policy framework that would apply to all entities of the Abu Dhabi government. With regard to environmental topics, it included the establishment of a separate committee for "infrastructure and environment", which set guidelines for environmental, health and safety such as the vision to become "a leader in green technologies" and to "diversify the national energy mix" (The

Abu Dhabi Executive Council 2007: 9, 54). Furthermore, as part of the 2030 economic vision, the Executive Council announced the launch of the Masdar initiative (hereafter: Masdar) in April 2006. Developed as an "alternative energy project" (ibid.: 54), its objective was two-pronged: Although created to respond to the global need of alternative energy sources and to underpin Abu Dhabi's long-term position as a reliable global energy provider (ibid.: 55), Masdar's primary target was to diversify the UAE's own energy and technology supply. Masdar contains four key targets:

1. Contribute to the economic diversification of Abu Dhabi;
2. Maintain, and later expand, Abu Dhabi's position in evolving global energy markets;
3. Position Abu Dhabi as a developer of technology rather than an importer;
4. Make a meaningful contribution towards sustainable human development.

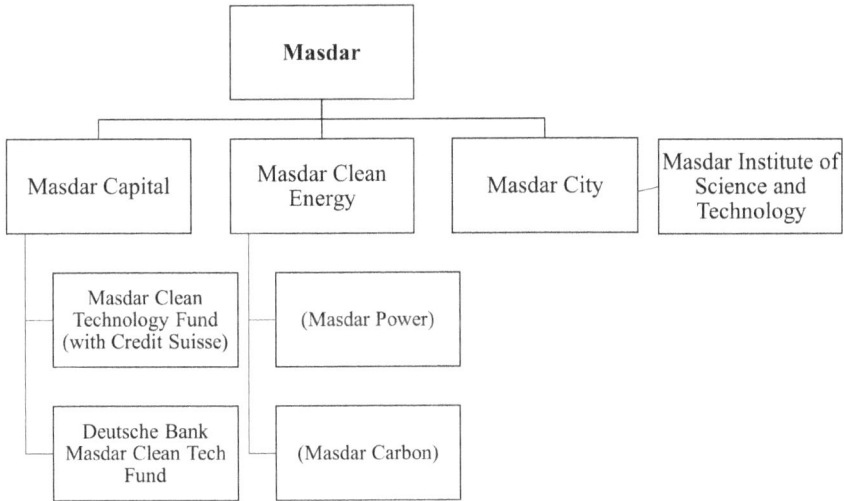

Source: Own illustration.
Fig. 1: Masdar's business units

Masdar, equivalent to the Abu Dhabi Future Energy Company, is a subsidiary of the government-owned Mubadala Investment Company and has comprised three business units since its establishment: Masdar Capital, Masdar Clean Energy and Masdar City. In addition, it formerly oversaw the Masdar Institute of Science and Technology (Table 1). The Masdar entities aim to develop and integrate the renewable and clean technology lifecycle, from research to overseas investment

(Low 2012: 31). First, Masdar Capital comprises two funds, the Masdar Clean Technology Fund, launched in 2006 in partnership with Credit Suisse, and the Deutsche Bank Masdar Clean Tech Fund which was established in 2009. According to UAE sources, they aim to promote and commercialize renewable technologies (UAE-US 2020a). In its initiation phase, the Masdar Clean Technology Fund was established with funding of 250 million US dollars, investing 45 million US dollars in three clean-tech funds and the rest in 12 companies as lead or co-lead investor (Bloomberg 2019). The projects are conducted in the fields of renewable energy and sustainability (Low 2012: 33).

Furthermore, Masdar Clean Energy develops large-scale energy and technology projects that enhance renewable power generation. In line with Masdar Capital's focus, the Masdar Clean Energy projects include alternative-energy power plants such as concentrating solar power (CSP), solar photovoltaic (PV), wind energy and waste to energy plants (UAE-US 2020a). At an early project stage, Masdar Clean Energy incorporated the business units of Masdar Power and Masdar Carbon (Low 2012: 33f). However, neither the government of Abu Dhabi nor official publications by Masdar refer to business units other than Masdar Clean Energy. According to the Masdar Clean Energy fact sheet (Masdar 2019c), it has a portfolio of domestic and international renewable power generation projects of 8.5 billion US dollars; Masdar's share of this investment is 2.7 billion US dollars.

As previously mentioned, Masdar City was initiated as a planned eco-city project, situated six kilometers from the Abu Dhabi airport. Launched in April 2006, it was designed by the British architectural design and engineering studio Foster + Partners and originally envisioned to cover six square kilometers. Construction began in 2008 and the first buildings were completed in 2010. Doulet (2016: 125) explains that the actual construction in that first phase was conducted by partner companies of Foster + Partners due to the studio's financial downturn during the financial crisis in 2008/09. Masdar City was founded to create an urban space targeting reducing energy, water and waste and thus becoming a carbon-neutral city to accommodate 50,000 people for living and 40,000 people for work and study (Masdar 2017: 2). Apart from that, it aimed to attract more than 1,500 companies and research institutions in the field of sustainable energy technologies (Reiche 2010a: 2419). Scholars refer to differing planned end dates of the project: Whereas Reiche (Reiche 2010a, 2010b) explains that construction originally was supposed to end in 2016, I find 2030 as a final date in the analysis of Low (2012: 31), in line with the Abu Dhabi 2030 vision. In recent government sources, a possible end date is not cited.

The Masdar Institute of Science and Technology (MI) was initiated as a research institute and university in the field of information technology, water and, environment and engineering. Designed and built by Foster + Partners and established in 2007 in cooperation with the Massachusetts Institute of Technology (MIT), MI has provided academic programs in information technology, water and environment, engineering systems and management, material sciences and engineering and mechanical engineering for graduate students (Reiche 2010b: 379). Its first class graduated in 2011 (Low 2012: 31). In 2017, MI merged with the Khalifa University of Science, Technology and Research (KUSTAR) and the Petroleum Institute (PI), today altogether renamed into The Khalifa University of Science and Technology (KU). According to the KU website, the MI's responsibilities lie with the sustainability-focused research centers. It offers graduate students the possibility to acquire practical skills through its "partnership with local and international organizations" (KU 2018). As Atalay et al. (2016: 209) point out, MI illustrates a clear example of international research collaboration. Masdar's institutional research structure mirrors that of an "important body of MIT, the MIT energy initiative, a specialized research hub, which aims to develop breakthrough energy technologies […] to provide a more sustainable future at the global level" (ibid.). In addition, the MI integrates the research divisions of technology development and renewable energy. In this regard, it founded the world's first university for artificial intelligence (AI) located in Masdar City which began offering courses in September 2020.

5 Ecological modernization in the UAE through the lens of Masdar City

5.1 Masdar technology

Science and technology play a key role in the technological transformation associated with the concept of ecological modernization. In this context, I analyze Masdar's focus on the development and innovation of renewable energy, as well as other sectors including green and sustainable building, transportation and carbon capture, storage, and utilization.

5.1.1 Renewable energy

Since the initiation of the Masdar initiative in 2006, Masdar has established and invested in several projects which enhance the production of renewable energy. According to official sources (Masdar 2020a), it has developed projects in 30 countries, which produce an overall amount of approximately 6 GW gross. When comparing the UAE to other countries of the GCC, the UAE accounts for the largest share (68 percent) of renewable energy capacity in 2018 (IRENA 2019: 49). Solar PV and CSP dominate the current installed renewable energy capacity within Masdar's portfolio (Figure 2). Amongst them, "Shams 1", located in Abu Dhabi and operating at an energy capacity of 100 MW (see Table 2), is the first CSP plant among all GCC countries (ibid.: 56). Masdar also developed and co-developed other solar PV projects on a large scale, such as the third phase of the Mohammed bin Rashid Al Maktoum Solar Park in Dubai (planned to cover 800 MW of solar PV capacity and be fully operational by 2020) or the Noor Abu Dhabi ("Sweihan") plant in Abu Dhabi, which was auctioned for 1,177 MW (Masdar 2020a). Besides solar power resources, Masdar has been innovative in waste-to-energy technology. According to official sources, the recently established facility in Sharjah has an installed net power of 30 MW and processes more than 300,000 tons of municipal solid waste per year. It is planned to be operational in the third quarter of 2021. According to IRENA (2019: 57), the project has been introduced in the course of Sharjah's governmental zero-waste landfill target to divert waste from landfills by 100 percent by 2015 (UAE Government 2019) and the UAE's target to divert waste from landfills by 75 percent by 2021 ("UAE Government's Vision 2021", ibid.).

https://doi.org/10.1515/9783110749298-005

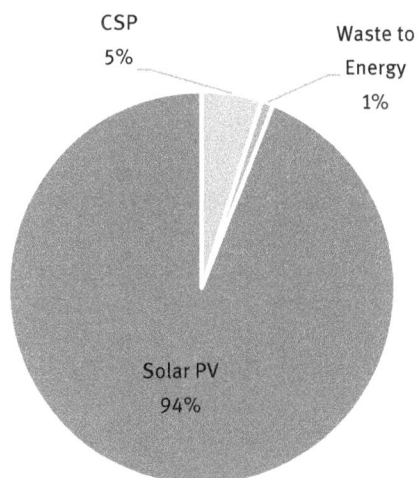

Source: Own illustration.
Fig. 2: Share of total energy generated in the UAE by Masdar

Tab. 2: Masdar renewable energy projects in the UAE by technology
Source: Own illustration, data based on Masdar (2020a).

Technology	Project	Capacity (MW)
Solar PV	Abu Dhabi Solar Rooftop Program	0.02
	Abu Dhabi Al Jarnain Island PV Plant	0.75
	Masdar City Solar Photovoltaic Plant	10
	Abu Dhabi Murawah Island	0.5
	Noor Abu Dhabi, Sweihan	1177
	Abu Dhabi Sea Palace	0.2
	Abu Dhabi Um Al Zomul	0.1
	Dubai Mohammed bin Rashid Al Maktoum Solar Park, Phase III	800
	Ras Al Khaimah Omran Hospital	0.45
CSP	Abu Dhabi Shams 1	100
Waste-to-energy	Sharjah Waste-to-Energy Project	30

Besides projects on a domestic level, Masdar participates in 41 projects outside the UAE with a total energy capacity of approximately 4 GW gross.[8] Two projects have attracted international attention based on their wind energy capacity. "London Array", opened in 2013 and located on the Thames Estuary, presents one of the "largest offshore wind farms in the world", covering 175 wind turbines at a capacity of 630 MW in total (Masdar 2020a). In addition, Masdar has a 25 percent share in the "Hywind" windfarm located off the coast in Aberdeenshire in Scotland. According to promotional material provided by Masdar (ibid.), it presents the "first integrated energy storage system in the world to be connected to a floating offshore wind farm", covering up to an installed capacity of 30 MW. 63 percent of the energy generated by projects with Masdar's participation is produced by wind energy (Figure 4).

This data demonstrates that Masdar has certainly lived up to the official narrative of the Abu Dhabi Policy Agenda 2007/08. Large-scale domestic solar PV projects have increased the share of renewable energy supply in the national market, and projects such as the waste-to-energy facility in Sharjah have demonstrated a UAE interest in developing renewable technology. In this regard, Masdar's engagement in renewable energy can also be understood as the outcome of the Abu Dhabi strategy to increase economic diversification. As Luomi (2009: 108) explains, Abu Dhabi officials "aimed at diversifying Abu Dhabi's fossil-fuel-based rentier state", in which renewable energy revenues boost the diversification of the UAE's economic dependence on fossil fuel revenues. At the same time, Masdar's investment in and co-development of projects outside the UAE stresses its international visibility. The Masdar project has put the UAE on the "global map" of renewable energy, both as a supplier as well as a pioneering developer (ibid.: 107). As Atalay et al. (2016: 209) state, the UAE stands out with its "ambitious" renewable energy projects, which make it the leader among the GCC states in renewable energy adoption.

---

8 Recent projects include a 200 MW solar project outside Baku, Azerbaijan, and a 100 MW solar plant and a 500 MW wind project in the Navoi region in Uzbekistan (Bridge 2020; Masdar 2020g, 2020h).

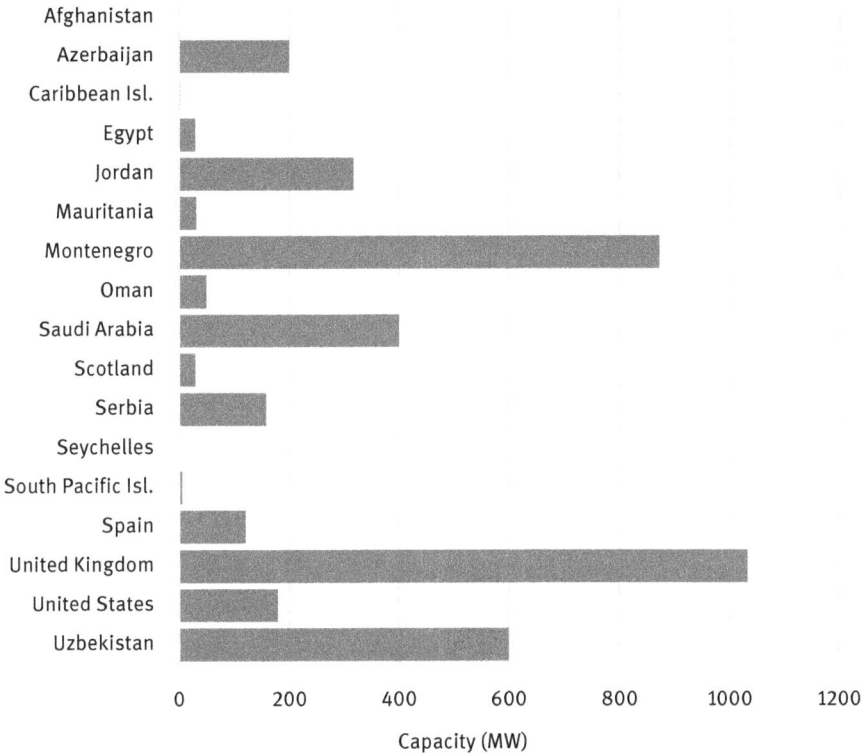

Source: Own illustration, data based on Masdar (2020a).
Fig. 3: Masdar projects worldwide

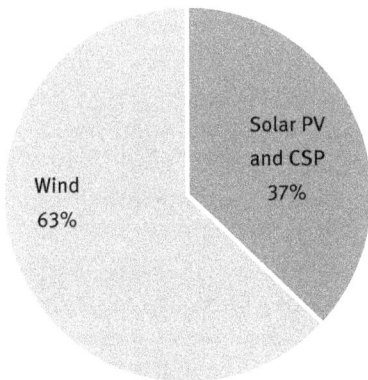

Source: Own illustration.
Fig. 4: Share of total energy generated worldwide by Masdar

5.1.2 Green building, transportation and carbon capture utilization and storage

In the course of eco-city and sustainable city projects, green or "sustainable" con-struction and building has been a major focus of research and development. Green building is defined as "the practice of creating structures and using pro-cesses that are environmentally responsible and resource-efficient throughout a building's life-cycle from siting to design, construction, operation, maintenance, renovation and deconstruction" (US EPA 2016). As Doukas et al. (2006: 767) high-light, the building sector in the UAE represents a very energy-intensive sector, as the average energy use per area in domestic buildings is high and public build-ings show "less sustainable measures in terms of energy features, energy perfor-mance [and] environmental features and privacy" (ibid.). In contrast, according to Masdar (2019a), Masdar City implemented green building material which re-duces water and energy use. Moreover, buildings in Masdar City must meet a spe-cific rating according to the "Estidama Pearl Building Rating System". Estidama was established in 2010 by the Abu Dhabi Department of Urban Planning and Municipalities, aiming to create sustainable communities, cities and global en-terprises on the basis of the four pillars environment, economy, culture and soci-ety (Abu Dhabi UPC 2016: 1). According to official sources, Pearl conforms to the green building rating system "Leadership in Energy and Environmental Design" (LEED) developed by the United States Green Building Council (USGBC) (Masdar 2019a). Nevertheless, Cugurullo (2013a: 33) emphasizes the lack of official data published by Masdar City on the actual performance of the green building initia-tive: According to him, independent and public verification has been performed on an official basis, however, "no outsider" has yet been able to verify the prom-ised figures. Moreover, by applying a local certification scheme such as Pearl, the Abu Dhabi government clearly enhanced the promotion of national development and innovation initiatives in green and sustainable building. As Gilley (2012: 298) asserts, the application of international green building certification would re-quire third-party gatherings of information "so that building owners, renters, prospective purchasers, civil society groups, lawyers and investigative journal-ists can monitor actual building performance".

Masdar City has also developed and implemented a driverless city transport system. The personal rapid transit (PRT) has run since 2010 and, according to Masdar's promotional material (2020b), pursues "a transportation strategy on a hierarchy that puts pedestrians first and emphasizes sustainable, public transportation [...] with clean point-to-point services".[9] PRT presents a concept of personalized urban mass transit, developed in the 1960s,[10] where PRT vehicles seat two to six passengers like conventional automobiles. When evaluated from a technical perspective, the Masdar PRT system has the potential to support all its projected "internal transit needs" (ibid.: 268). This means that all intra-urban spaces are accessible by PRT vehicles and meet the demand.[11] Besides the PRT system, Masdar is developing an integrated freight system, the freight rapid transit (FRT), operating on the same infrastructure as PRT (Mueller/Sgouridis 2011: 268). As with the case of the Pearl certification, very little information is published on the PRT system in official publications. However, Abbasi et al. (2012: 12) assess that battery-operated vehicles, as is the case for the PRT, emit arguably more carbon dioxide emissions net than fuel-efficient, gas-driven cars. Masdar City thus can only be "carbon-neutral" by transportation "in the sense that [..] emissions generated due to its construction and functioning will not be emitted [on] its premises, but some distance away from it" (ibid.). Moreover, Cugurullo (2013a: 29) adds that in 2013, the PRT, originally planned to cover the whole surface of the development, was limited to less than 10 percent of the Masdar project area while electric cars were allowed to drive freely within the city. Therefore, he argues that Masdar's PRT system failed in its main objective to "separate people from transports".

In addition, in 2006, Masdar co-developed with the Abu Dhabi National Oil Company (ADNOC) the first carbon capture utilization and storage (CCUS) project in the Middle East, named Al Reyadah. It was presented as the first facility to capture carbon dioxide emissions from the iron and steel industry while being one of 22 large-scale CCUS ventures worldwide (Masdar 2016a). As Nader (2009: 3954) explains, Masdar projected CCUS to be "the technology most likely to quickly deliver large-scale reductions in anthropogenic carbon dioxide emissions".[12] Unlike the green building certification and PRT, Masdar's CCUS project should be considered in the wider context of international climate action. The objective of the core project of Masdar's Clean Energy unit is to significantly mitigate the UAE's climate impact by capturing, reusing and storing 800,000 tons of CO_2 (Masdar 2016a). In this context, Masdar aims to attract and link CCUS to the Kyoto Clean Development Mechanism (CDM) to obtain tradeable carbon dioxide emission

---

9 See Mueller and Sgouridis (2011) for a technical assessment of Masdar's PRT system.

10 The concept initially was introduced by Fichter (1964).

11 The system works by demand. Simulation models estimated that it has to cover an area with 50,000 inhabitants (Mueller/Sgouridis 2011: 254).

12 See Nader (2009) for a profound technical discussion of the Abu Dhabi CCUS project.

credits both on the domestic and international market (Luomi 2009: 107; Theeyattuparampil et al. 2013: 302). In doing so, Masdar is expected to enhance the UAE's positioning as a relevant actor in the development and innovation of climate mitigation strategies. In addition, the CCUS project illustrated new economic opportunities for Masdar to attract potential investors (Theeyattuparampil et al. 2013: 298). Moreover, it opened up new partnerships in research and development and in knowledge-sharing with internationally renowned research institutes (such as the MIT in the case of CCUS), universities, organizations, forums and technology-focused companies (ibid.: 297). Eventually, it seemed to create an avenue for the UAE government to develop credibility and political legitimacy on both domestically and internationally. Accordingly, the UAE leaders could show a strong interest in the establishment of a "clean" fossil-fuel based economy and national commitment towards international climate targets.

5.2 Economic aspects

When analyzing Masdar City through the lens of ecological modernization, this theoretical grounding assumed that certain assignments, incentives and tasks are transferred from the state level to the market and economic agents. Moreover, global market dynamics and market actors influence the interdependence of economy and environment. On the basis of the Masdar City case, I examine the role of sovereign wealth funds (SWFs), economic diversification and international trade.

5.2.1 Sovereign wealth funds

Abu Dhabi attracted international scholarly and policymaking attention when in the mid-2000s, GCC-based SWFs arose (Ulrichsen 2017: 103). Sovereign wealth funds are business enterprises under full or partial state ownership (Kowalski et al. 2013: 10; The World Bank 2006: 7). A sovereign wealth fund represents one specific type of government-owned investment institution (Bazoobandi 2013: 17). According to the Sovereign Wealth Fund Institute (SWFI 2020a),[13] it is "a state-

---

13 Alternatively, Rozanov (2005: 52) explains that SWFs are set up in order to "insulate the budget and economy from excess volatility in revenues, help monetary authorities sterilize unwanted liquidity, build up savings for future generations, or use the money for economic and social development".

owned investment fund or entity that is commonly established from [the] balance of payments surpluses, official foreign currency operations, the proceeds of privatizations, governmental transfer payments, fiscal surpluses and/or receipts resulting from resource exports". Most SWFs are situated in states that are well equipped with fossil fuel deposits and further natural resources (Reiche 2010c: 3569). Formally, SWFs are public institutions, but they work like private actors (Richardson 2011: 1). Moreover, they imply a "different kind of reassertion of state authority in the market[s]", which positions them close to policy issues (Sun et al. 2014: 655). SWFs seek long-term returns, and societal benefits rather than short-term cost benefits. Hence, energy has been a "favorite sector" for SWF investment because of limited supply and long-term profitability (ibid.: 654).

The Abu Dhabi Investment Authority (ADIA) constitutes the largest SWF (in total assets) among the GCC countries, and the third largest SWF worldwide (SWFI 2020b). Founded in 1976, it replaced the Abu Dhabi Financial Investment Board and has been owned and operated by the emirate's government through the Abu Dhabi Investment Council (ADIC). ADIA is regulated by UAE federal law (number 5, 1981, see Ulrichsen 2017: 103) which authorizes ADIA to invest on behalf of the Abu Dhabi government. It is led by sheikh Khalifa bin Zayed Al Nahyan as the chairman, ruler of Abu Dhabi and president of the UAE, while his half-brothers sheikh Mohammed bin Zayed and sheikh Mansour bin Zayed held roles at the two leading SWFs in Abu Dhabi, the Mubadala Development Corporation and the International Petroleum Investment Company (IPIC) respectively. In 2017, the Mubadala Development Corporation and IPIC merged and established the Mubadala Investment Company (hereafter: Mubadala). Mubadala is another sovereign wealth fund wholly owned by the Abu Dhabi government (Mubadala 2020a). It concentrates on investment in capital intensive industries such as healthcare, semiconductor computer chip manufacturing, aerospace, and renewable energy (Ulrichsen 2017: 104). Bazoobandi (2013: 83) highlights a significant overlap of high-ranking officials, who sit in the advisory boards of both ADIA and the other SWFs (Table 3 gives an overview of ADIA and Mubadala). Hence, Abu Dhabi's investment is mostly held in sovereign wealth funds and other investment vehicles, which concentrate on maximizing the emirate's "comparative advantage" (Ulrichsen 2017: 108) in the energy sector. By investing heavily in renewable energy, Abu Dhabi provides a case study "in how a determined leadership campaign dovetailed with the ready availability of investment resources to reposition the UAE in [...] international energy governance" (ibid.: 114).

Tab. 3: Abu Dhabi sovereign wealth enterprises
Source: Own illustration, based on ADIA (2020); Mubadala (2020b); SWFI (2020b).

Profile	ADIA	Mubadala
Establishment	1976	2017, through merging IPIC (1984) and Mubadala Development Company (2002)
Assets (in billion US dollars)	580*	232
Investment focus	Indexed funds, fixed income and treasury, real estate and infrastructure, equities and private equities	Alternative investments and infrastructure, technology, manufacturing and mining, petroleum and petrochemicals, aerospace, renewables, information and communication
Board of Directors	Sheikh Khalifa bin Zayed Al Nahyan (Chair) Sheikh Mohamed bin Zayed Al Nahyan (Deputy Chair) Sheikh Hamed bin Zayed Al Nahyan (Managing Director) Sheikh Mansour bin Zayed Al Nahyan Sheikh Mohammed bin Khalifa bin Zayed Al Nahyan Mohammed Habroush Al Suwaidi Khalil Mohammed Sharif Foulathi	Sheikh Mohamed bin Zayed Al Nahyan (Chair) Sheikh Mansour bin Zayed Al Nahyan (Deputy Chair) Khaldoon Khalifa Al Mubarak (Managing Director) Mohammed Ahmed Al Bowardi Suhail Mohamed Faraj Al Mazrouei Abdulhamid Saeed Mahmood Ebraheem Al Mahmood

* According to Bazoobandi (2013: 131f), most of the information on the size of ADIA's assets is based on speculation as the fund avoids officially disclosing information on its activities to the public.

In line with Sun et al. (2014), Abu Dhabi's SWFs have thus emerged as important actors within policy decisions in the emirate. The implementation of Masdar City by a government-related enterprise contrasts with assumptions made in the concept of ecological modernization: Whereas scholars presume a shift from state to private institutions, SWFs are public institutions that act as private companies. Moreover, in this case, all sovereign wealth management institutions are managed directly by members of the ruling families and individuals close to them. Therefore, transparency in operation and governance of these organizations presents a controversial issue. More precisely, there is little difference within the management of the private and national wealth, that is the "blurry line between the ruling figure's personal properties and the country's national wealth" (Bazoobandi 2013: 175). Furthermore, the development and core projects in Masdar City are entirely dependent on the ruling families' confidence and financing: Without Abu Dhabi's oil revenues, combined with the small number of UAE citizens involved in the rentier bargain, Masdar would have never materialized (Luomi 2009: 108).

5.2.2 Economic diversification and international trade

Both governmental and scholarly literature (see for instance El-Kharouf et al. 2010; Haouas/Heshmati 2014; Hvidt 2013; Shayah 2015) embed the establishment of Masdar City in the context of Abu Dhabi's economic diversification policy, as laid down in its 2007/08 policy agenda. In political economy, "diversification normally refers to exports, and specifically to policies aiming to reduce the dependence on a limited number of export commodities that may be subject to price and volume fluctuations or secular declines" (Routledge Encyclopedia 2001: 360). For El-Kharouf et al. (2010: 135) economic diversification in GCC countries also attempts to overcome problems such as low growth rates, lack of public and private incentives to accumulate human capital, lack of competitiveness, the likelihood of shocks and spill-over effects in the economies and various rentier effects.[14] In order to push diversification, the UAE emirates gradually began to develop areas of specialist expertise in niche sectors. After Dubai had diversified its economy at a very early stage, Abu Dhabi long existed in a "near-parallel" economy, that was the coexistence of Abu Dhabi's resources-rich energy sector and the non-resource economies of Dubai and the other five emirates (Ulrichsen 2017: 87).

However, in the early 2000s, Abu Dhabi began to diversify its economy by shifting the focus to the renewable and clean technology sector. According to Madichie (2011: 42), Masdar presents a "business case" of Abu Dhabi's economic diversification strategy: Through the development of a knowledge-based clean energy sector, the UAE sought to position itself in the development of com-

---

14 The secretariat to the UNFCCC (2016: 13) has highlighted another dimension of the objective of economic diversification for non-Annex I parties (such as the GCC countries). Economic diversification hence is included in the development plans to implement mitigation policies. In this context, countries with a narrow export profile "are highly vulnerable to response measures owing to new demands or standards from importers".

mercially viable, sustainable energy solutions.[15] Moreover, Luomi (2009: 108) explains that with regard to energy policy, Masdar presented the largest investment cluster in renewable energy and other alternatives to fossil fuels in the region. It increased the UAE's comparative advantages achieved through long-term experience in the fossil fuel industry and the scaling up of technologies. Masdar City implemented a free and investment zone for international companies, small and medium-sized enterprises and start-ups (Masdar 2020d). As Khodr and Reiche (2012: 155) state, such a free zone offers companies multiple economic incentives, opportunities, and benefits and provides "governmentally user-friendly" services. Thereby, Masdar describes it itself as a "good practice" example for a free trade zone: Offering a "100 percent ownership, 100 percent exemption for corporate and personal income taxes, zero import tariffs, a quick and easy set-up for registration, government relations and visa processing, freedom of repatriation of capital and profits" as well as the access to sector knowledge and talent pool (Masdar 2020d). As Mascarenhas (2018: 140) underlines, free zones have been commonly established among the GCC states and proved to be economically viable and simultaneously attracting global, regional and local stakeholders.

Tab. 4: UAE foreign direct investment (FDI) overview, 2005-2018
Source: Own illustration, based on UNCTAD (2019).

Year	Inward FDI (in million US dollars)	Outward FDI (in million US dollars)
2005-2007*	12,631	9,737
2011	7,679	2,178
2015	8,551	16,692
2016	9,605	15,711
2017	10,354	14,060
2018	10,385	15,079

* Pre-financial crisis annual average.

---

15 To enlarge its energy mix, the UAE initiated a nuclear energy program in 2007 with the first reactors built in 2012 (Ulrichsen 2017: 118). Yet "clean" in terms of polluted carbon dioxide emissions, I clearly delimit nuclear power from renewable energy resources, for its high costs and the risks it poses to health and safety.

In fact, Masdar represents a free zone which is a catalyst for foreign direct investment (FDI), innovation and public-private partnerships "attempting to move beyond traditional foreign investment restrictions in [..] authoritarian states" (Mascarenhas 2018: 140). In 2015, the FDI inward flow to the UAE was 8,551 million US dollars (Table 4). The total value of FDI for the principality of Abu Dhabi accounted approximately 27 percent of the total UAE FDI inward flow (SCAD 2018: 67).[16] In this context, Masdar turned out to be a global "hub" connecting local, regional and international companies with a specialization in renewable energy.

The most prominent examples of firms and organizations present in Masdar City include regional offices of General Electric, the Middle East headquarters of Siemens, and the headquarters of IRENA (Masdar 2020d). In 2009, it was decided to establish IRENA in Masdar City. According to Luomi (2009: 113), the UAE presented strong arguments: IRENA would be the first global agency in the Middle East and the Masdar project itself should serve as proof of Abu Dhabi's commitment towards IRENA's targets and activities. Also, Abu Dhabi and Masdar City could set an example for other Global South countries in the development and promotion of renewable energy and other environmental innovation and technologies. Furthermore, both Ulrichsen (2017: 117) and Luomi (2009: 113) note the largesse of Masdar's financial offer. This included the coverage of all building and operating costs of IRENA as well as an allowance for conference facilities and staff visa costs. The financial promises totaled 135 million US dollars with another 50 million US dollars annual loans through the Abu Dhabi Fund for Development (ADFD) for IRENA projects in the Global South for the period from 2009 to 2015 (Luomi 2009: 114).[17] Winning IRENA for Masdar City certainly was a benchmark for the UAE government to position itself on the global map of renewable energy: From an economic perspective, it led to the attraction of international investors and private actors in this sector. Moreover, it resulted in an increased attention by policymakers on the international level, who, as far as they were represented in IRENA, were "expected to keep a watchful eye on the progress of the developments around them" (Reiche 2010b: 381).

---

16 Due to lack of data on the FDI inward flow to Masdar City, I excluded a detailed FDI analysis in my work.

17 To compare, the offer of the competing country Germany included only 6 million US dollars for setting up the agency and another 3-4 million US dollars for annual operating costs.

5.3 Institutional framework

As the concept of ecological modernization presumes, emerging institutional structures which create a system of dealing with environmental issues carry out and transform environmental policy. In this study, I intend to embed urban governance structures in federal and state environmental policy. My analysis includes the private department of the ruling family, governmental institutions and the role of public enterprises.

5.3.1 The private departments of sheikh Zayed and his successors

Many projects in the field of ecology and environment are the outcome of personal convictions of UAE's founding father, sheikh Zayed. Sheikh Zayed originally initiated a "greening" of the country. This referred to a national strategy of modernization by transforming parts of the country's desert landscapes into green areas by devoting enormous resources to agricultural development, park landscaping, and nature reserves (Ouis 2002a: 334; see also Section 5.5). The projects were conducted by the private department of sheikh Zayed, named the "Environment and Wildlife Management Department", and established in 1996. In its beginning, the department focused on the protection of game such as the Arabian oryx or the hubara bustard (Ouis 2002b: 304). However, modeled on the private department of sheikh Zayed, crown prince sheikh Khalifa and sheikhs of the other emirates individually built their private organizations. As Al Qatami (1995: 243) states, the efforts of the private departments of sheikh Zayed and his successors have "serve[d] the objective of maintaining the ecological balance in the UAE and at the regional and international levels, in accordance with the Agreement on Biological Diversity".

In Masdar City, for instance, the private department of sheikh Mohamed leads the Abu Dhabi Sustainability Week (ADSW), which is a yearly conference established in 2008. ADSW aims to create a platform of knowledge exchange in the fields of energy and climate change, water, mobility, space, biotechnology and other technological innovation (Masdar 2020e). In addition to that, sheikh Mohammed bin Rashid Al Maktoum, vice president and prime minister of the UAE and ruler of Dubai, initiated the Zayed International Foundation for the Environment, which awards the "Zayed International Prize for the Environment", recognizing environmental achievements which support and promote environmental projects aligned to the UN Sustainable Development Goals (SDGs) (Zayed International 2020). As Heard-Bey (1982: 406) explains, the importance of the leaders' private departments is that these are "institutions of traditional power".

Therefore, the sheikhs have always been considered the "owners of the land", and they have always held the power to modify institutions, policies and processes "as they please" (Ouis 2002b: 304).

5.3.2 Governmental institutions

The political and institutional foundation for environmental policy in the UAE includes several elements of the framework presented by Jörgens (1996). Accordingly, UAE environmental policy is conducted on the federal level by a ministry, environmental law and an environmental report, usually accompanied by some kind of expert committee or working group. Table 5 gives an overview of environmental institutional structure in the UAE. However, the following analysis concentrates on those institutions which shape environmental decision-making for Masdar City.

Although environmental policy-making power lies with the emirates (see Section 4.1), Masdar City applies the common UAE environmental law on the "protection and development of the environment" (federal law number 24, 1999). This law sets the regulations for the protection and conservation of the quality of the environment. It regulates all forms of pollution and protects the development of natural resources and the conservation of biological diversity. It ensures the protection of society and the state from activities that are "environmentally harmful" in compliance with international and regional conventions regarding environmental issues. The federal environmental law was introduced in 1999 by the Federal Environment Agency (FEA), which merged with the national Ministry of Environment and Water (MOEW) in 2006 (MOCCAE 2018). In 2016, MOEW was renamed into the Ministry of Climate Change and Environment (MOCCAE), which today is the UAE ministry for climate and environmental topics and is responsible for all legislative preparations, environmental law and environmental programs (MOCCAE 2018). As part of MOCCAE, the UAE Council for Climate Change and Environment formulates the UAE's environmental policy and has a representative function on the regional and international level (MOCCAE decision number 795, 2016). The federal governmental bodies frame policies for the development of environmental protection measures. These policies are enacted by the individual emirates according to their local environmental strategies. Furthermore, the emirates have established local regulatory agencies to oversee and implement sector-specific environmental activities (Thacker/SK 2021: 1).

In the emirate of Abu Dhabi, the Environment Agency Abu Dhabi (EAD), established in 1996 as the Environmental Research and Wildlife Development

Agency (ERWDA) is responsible for environmental issues. Its main objective is the protection of the natural environment, wildlife and biological diversity through monitoring and the submission of proposals and recommendations (law number 4, 1996: Article 3). Furthermore, the key piece of EAD's environmental legislation is law number 21, 2005, which deals with waste management in the emirate and forms the legal basis for Masdar City's strategy on waste (Masdar 2012: 37; 94). In addition to that, Masdar is included in the environmental strategy of EAD (2017: 29), which depicts Masdar as the country's leading "driver" in research and development. Masdar City is considered an independent entity: It is subject to EAD law and regulations and collaborates with EAD in working groups or expert committees in the topics of climate change and sustainability (such as Masdar ExCom, Masdar 2012: 22).

Tab. 5: Environmental institutional structure in the UAE
Source: Own illustration.

Institution/Level	Function/Link to Masdar City
Ruling family	
The sheikhs' private departments for environmental concerns	– Sheikhs' preferences determine environmental policy-making – Law-enforcing decrees reflect individual preferences (Aspinall 2001: 289) – Established the Abu Dhabi Sustainability Week (ADSW) or the "Zayed International Prize for the Environment" (Masdar City)
Federal level	
UAE Ministry of Climate Change and Environment (MOCCAE)	– Built on the Supreme Committee for Environment (1975) and FEA (1993) – Formerly the Ministry of Environment and Water (MOEW) (2006-2016) – Responsible for legislation, environmental law, programs, research and executive functions
Federal Environment Agency (FEA)	– Established under federal law number 7 (1993) – Moved to MOCCAE under federal law number 7 (2009) – Responsible for the preparation and implementation of main environmental law, federal law number 24 (1999)
Federal law number 24 (1999)	– Regulates the protection and conservation of the quality and natural balance of the environment and biological diversity – Complies with international and regional environmental conventions (Article 2) – Force of law to Masdar City
UAE Environment Report	– Published by MOCCAE since 2014

Institution/Level	Function/Link to Masdar City
Emirate level	
Environment Agency Abu Dhabi (EAD)	– Established under law 16 (2005) – Replaced the Environmental Research and Wildlife Development Agency (ERWDA) – Responsible for the protection of the environment and wildlife with its biological diversity – Publishes recommendations and studies – Masdar City is subject to EAD law/Masdar and EAD collaborate through working groups/expert committees
Abu Dhabi Agriculture and Food Safety Authority (ADAFSA)	– Formerly the Food and Environmental Control Center (FECC) – Conducts practical environmental work in the fields of human health, food and recycling
Law number 21 (2005)	– Enhances waste management in the emirate (Article 2) – Basis for waste and recycle management in Masdar City
Abu Dhabi State of Environment Report	– Published every five years by EAD – Examines the environmental situation in Abu Dhabi from a technical and policy perspective – Latest report in 2017 cites Masdar as "a driver of knowledge" (EAD 2017: 123)

5.3.3 Public enterprises

Sovereign wealth funds heavily influence and determine the UAE economic policy by investing and doing business on behalf of the UAE government (see Section 5.2). In this context, Aspinall (2001: 291) explains that companies which are partially or fully owned and run by the government represent another driving force in institutional environmental matters.

For the case of Masdar City, relevant actors are Masdar and its parent company Mubadala. On the Mubadala website (Mubadala 2020a), little information is available on the company's link with Masdar regarding policy, legislation, and practices. Mubadala divides its investment projects in alternative investments (such as private equity or venture capital) and the investment fields of infrastructure, aerospace, renewables and information and communications technology, petroleum and petrochemicals and technology, manufacturing and mining. In what may seem an ironic twist, Mubadala's petroleum and petrochemicals unit regularly publishes a report on "Operating Responsibly" (for example Mubadala Petroleum 2017). In the report (ibid.: 2), it is stated that Mubadala Petroleum is governed "by policies, standards and procedures, including [our] 'quality, health, safety, security and the environment (QHSSE)'". According to Azadeh et al. (2008: 403), QHSSE belongs to management systems that offer organizations and companies approaches to set guidelines and regulations for the disciplines of health, safety and the environment. An environmental management system, for instance, provides a framework for an organization to achieve and sustain performance in corresponding environmental goals and in response to changing regulations and social, financial, economic and competitive pressures related to environmental risks. In this regard, Mubadala Petroleum wants to underline that it applies environmental standards such as ISO 14001 or OHSAS 18001 (Occupational Health and Safety Assessment Series) (Mubadala Petroleum 2017: 4).[18] Furthermore, Masdar has published a sustainability report on a yearly basis since 2012, which is built on the guidelines of the Global Reporting Initiative (GRI), established in 1997 and aiming to develop globally applicable guidelines for reporting on economic, environmental, and social performance of an organization or company.

5.4 Environmental groups

Ecological modernization scholars assume that the state's hierarchical, centralized, and top-down structure changes to a participatory, consensual, cooperative, and interactive form of governance, in which social groups are increasingly involved in public and private decision-making institutions. In the upcoming analysis, I will assess to what extent environmental groups on a domestic and transnational level affect environmental reform processes in Masdar City.

5.4.1 National organizations

On the domestic level, Ouis (2002b: 307) finds two groups which seem relevant in their goals, size and functioning to have an impact on UAE environmental policy: the Environment Friends Society (EFS) as well as the Emirates Environmental Group (EEG). EFS, established in 1991 under ministerial decree number 478,

---

18 Environmental standards are administrative regulations implemented for the treatment and maintenance of the environment, see Mol (2002: 104). ISO 14001 presents a management system which sets regulations on an organization's environmental performance; OHSAS 18001 refers to occupational health and safety.

concentrates on topics of environmental education and awareness.[19] It conducts projects such as environmental festivals and other practical activities on waste and environmental conservation. In Masdar City, it organizes for example a "green" running competition, which aims to increase the awareness of environmental topics (Masdar Free Zone 2020). However, Ouis (2002b: 307) underlines that membership in EFS requires active members to be UAE passport holders,[20] "noted for good behavior and commendable conduct [and] never subject to dismissal or suspended from practicing in any other club or society". Still, "affiliate membership" is open for members from non-UAE countries and the directorate of the EFS, closely linked to the ruling family, can award "honorary membership".

EEG, based in Dubai and established in 1991, has a similar focus on the promotion of environmental topics. All EEG projects, most of them concentrating on waste and recycling issues, are sponsored by the Dubai government and the Dubai municipality (ibid.: 308). Both groups, EFS and EEG, describe themselves as non-governmental organizations (NGOs) (see Aspinall 2001: 291; EEG 2020a). Yet, their structure and functioning resemble what Naím (2009: 222) describes as government-organized non-governmental organizations (GONGOs). GONGOs are governmentally funded non-governmental organizations, which vary in their intensity and influence. In some authoritarian states,[21] GONGOs "are far from weakening state power, [... but] actually are means of preserving and expanding state power". In this regard, they act as "agents of the governments that fund them" (ibid.). In this regard, Ouis (2002b: 307) states that their loyalty to the UAE political leadership provides an example of how environmental concern is determined by the UAE rulers. More precisely, environmental concern is strongly linked to terms of nationalism and an "education" of the population in certain environmental topics (see Section 5.5). Therefore, in the case of the UAE, the "role of the society is an educational one" (ibid.: 308), which aims to increase environmental awareness in the UAE and tends to form the UAE population in its environmental behavior.

---

19 For Bonnett (2000: 597), environmental education aims "to transmit from above environmentally 'good' attitudes and behaviors". Hence, if environmental norms and values are created and describe a "scale" to identify "good" environmental attitudes, it is defined by "environmental awareness".

20 This effectively excludes the high percentage of expatriates living in the UAE.

21 GONGOs also exist under democratic governments. An example from the USA is the National Endowment for Democracy (NED), which is a private non-profit organization created in 1983 to transnationally strengthen democratic institutions through non-governmental efforts. NED is funded by the US government (Naím 2009: 223).

5.4.2 International NGOs and the role of the WWF

Similar to the national level, only a few international environmental NGOs are active in the UAE, of which the WWF has been the most cited (see for example Luomi 2014; Reiche 2010a). Running 3000 projects worldwide that deal with climate and energy, food, forests, freshwater, oceans, wildlife, finance, governance and markets (WWF 2019a), the WWF opened a domestic project office in Abu Dhabi in 2001, followed by two other offices in the emirates Dubai and Sharjah (WWF 2019b). Similar to EFS and EEG, Emirates Nature-WWF (formerly the Emirates Wildlife Society (EWS)) is officially labeled as a NGO and presents itself as "one of few environmental NGO's legally established in the UAE that has a federal mandate" (Emirates Nature-WWF 2018: 15). This notwithstanding, Emirates Nature-WWF (ibid.) states: "Emirates Nature-WWF is governed in accordance with the articles of the Ministry of Social Affairs. Its board of directors consists of a chairman and board members, all of whom are UAE nationals who represent the private, public and NGO sectors". In addition to that, Emirates Nature-WWF reports to WWF International and operates in accordance with WWF's principles and guidelines.

Tab. 6: National and international NGOs with a permanent presence in the UAE
Source: Own illustration.

Organization	Topic	Link to the UAE government
National level		
Environment Friends Society (EFS)	Environmental education and awareness	Establishment and funding
Emirates Environmental Group (EEG)	Environmental education (focus on waste)	Establishment and funding
International level		
World Wide Fund For Nature (WWF)	Wilderness preservation; the reduction of human impact on the environment	Establishment and funding of the regional office (Emirates Nature-WWF)

Among these projects, Emirates Nature-WWF attempted to certify Masdar City according to the "One Planet Living" (hereafter: One Planet) label of WWF International and BioRegional, a sustainable development program concentrating on possibilities for humankind to live within ecological limits (WWF 2018: 6). One

Planet contains ten principles, which guide participating organizations to plan, implement and communicate their One Planet projects (BioRegional 2017). Moreover, according to Madichie (2011: 43), Masdar City was planned to become One Planet certified: initially, it attempted to implement state of the art renewable technologies (such as PV, CSP and waste-to-energy), optimizing water resources through water recycling and an overall reduction of water demand, providing a zero-waste lifestyle (through the reduction, reuse, recovery, and recycling of waste materials) and the transformation of urban transport (through the use of PRT). By 2013, however, the implementation of One Planet in Masdar City had faced several issues (Crot 2013: 2813). Accordingly, in June 2009, Masdar had not yet signed the One Planet action plan, because this plan did not only include ecological aspects in its framework, but also addresses the social dimension of sustainability. Yet, Masdar announced its commitment to One Planet in 2010 (Masdar 2010, based on Crot 2013: 2816). In this context, Crot finds that the framework published in the Masdar report differed from WWF's initial version. Hence, any reference to labor issues had been removed, while Masdar vaguely communicated that "Masdar ensures that the community's impact on other communities is positive: Masdar City is committed to helping the broader Abu Dhabi community, the UAE, the region and the world" (ibid.: 2817).[22]

In addition, Cugurullo (2013a: 28; 33) stresses that Masdar City's association with WWF brought the project the attention of numerous international organizations and environmental experts. However, Masdar, as in the case of the One Planet certification, shows that

> what stays at the forefront does not correspond with what stays at the core, and that image and nature do not reflect each other. By scratching the surface, the reality of the Masdar City project comes out. [...] Although independent and public verification of Masdar's City performance in meeting these standards is [..] one of the features [... of] the project, [...] no outsider has been able to verify the foundations of the claims (ibid.).

5.5 Environmental education and awareness

The concept of ecological modernization presumes changing discursive practices and ideology. Accordingly, increasing knowledge and information should result

---

22 I could not find any updated data on the One Plant certification of Masdar City in official Masdar material (Masdar 2020f) nor the database of the One Planet Network (2020b). However, the One Planet program has recently been under transformation to implement the UN SDGs, which, in turn, are met by Masdar (Masdar 2016b).

in an emerging "ecological consciousness", in which environmental facts become politicized and affect the public discourse. Yet considering the difficulty of lack of data on public opinion polls, the objective in this section is to examine a shift in discursive practices within the context of environmental education programs and sheikh Zayed's relation to nature.

5.5.1 Educational programs

In order to assess values, opinions, beliefs and ideology, scholars have used political polls and surveys. However, as Bunce and Wolchik (2010: 62) explain, in authoritarian regimes, like the UAE,

> popular sentiments are unusually hard to decipher, because public opinion polls are rare, often non-reliable, and/or limited in their circulation and because publics respond to stolen elections by participating less and less over time in the electoral process [...] which [has already been] manipulated in many cases by the regime, overrepresented by regime supporters and 'acquiescers'.

Therefore, none of the common surveys that are conducted on a regional or international scale refer to environmental topics or include the UAE as a case. The only public opinion institute with a permanent presence in the UAE was the US polling institute Gallup, founded in 1935. The office was closed in 2012, nevertheless, polls have been conducted from Gallup's headquarters in the USA after that. Gallup's polls on the UAE cover topics such as health, "well-being" and entrepreneurship (Gallup 2020). With regard to environmental opinions, values and topics, it published a report on the occasion of the UAE's 40th anniversary, for which field work was conducted between 2009 and 2011 (Gallup 2011). According to the study's title "A Success Story", it polled that "from [the] residents' perspective, the UAE does a good job with regard to the environment" (ibid.). Besides, UAE citizens responded positively to practical recycling work in Abu Dhabi and the initiation plans for Masdar City. 87 percent of UAE citizens were satisfied with the country's efforts to preserve the environment and respondents were increasingly satisfied with the air quality as well as water conditions.

Both topics, waste and recycling, as highlighted by the Gallup report, are identical with the priority topics in the environmental (education) programs of the Environment Friends Society and the Emirates Environmental Group (see Section 5.4). Moreover, I find that the UAE government, in collaboration with EFS, EGG or through Abu Dhabi's Environment Agency itself, initiates and promotes several events for UAE citizens on environmental topics. As mentioned above,

EFS, for example, organizes the "green run" in Masdar City. Furthermore, EEG plans and conducts projects in form of interactive workshops or conferences on issues of sustainable waste management, recycling, greening landscapes, and urbanity. These projects comply with the criteria of the One Planet Network (2020a), which supports the implementation of the UN SDGs. Moreover, Aspinall (2001: 301) underlines that EFS, EEG and EAD regularly publish a number of books, magazines and articles that provide information about environmental issues. Apart from that, the UAE has celebrated the national "Environment Day" on fourth of February every year since 1997. Dedicating the celebrations to the founding day of the former Federal Environment Agency, the day is accompanied by much publicity, pre-, post- and same-day-events (Aspinall 2001: 301; MOCCAE 2017). Hence, the UAE government sponsors and promotes environmental awareness through the effective work of GONGOs. Moreover, by differentiating between a "good" and a "bad" environmental behavior of UAE citizens (see Section 5.4), the UAE government pursues a deliberate strategy to educate and "form" the UAE population in the selected topics.

Most initiatives and projects relate to and target young people. For instance, EEG conducts recycling challenges, environmental drawing workshops and other initiatives that aim to educate and make topics such as environmental preservation and sustainable development visible. According to promotional material, EEG's "educational programs arm the young minds with knowledge on sustainability and foster their responsibility, observation and awareness" (EEG 2020b). The youth here is described as "the backbone of the nation, to adapt long-lasting and persistent environmentally-friendly practices to be carried out into adulthood" (ibid.). In addition, EEG aims to include and engage students from other Arab countries in the region. This strongly resembles the concept of a "diffusion" process of values and norms, through which the Arab countries of the Persian Gulf gain regional influence (Kazerouni 2017: 91). Moreover, according to the "Connect with Nature" survey by YouGov, which was conducted in 2019 and included 500 people between the age of 18 to 29 years, 65 percent of the respondents want to protect the environment by participating in events and activities that benefit the environment. In addition to that, 70 percent wish to have access to more information about ways how to become environmentally active (Emirates Nature-WWF 2019).

5.5.2 Green Zayedism

According to Ouis (2002a, 2002b), sheikh Zayed and his relation to nature im-
printed changing discourses and ideology in the UAE concerning ecological values and beliefs (see also Section 5.3). Under Zayed's rule, the Emirati population
only cultivated areas close to the oases and in the mountains, by using irrigation
measures and technologies that required an intensive long-term engagement by
the government. This strategy, described as "rolling back the desert" (Ouis 2002a:
337), was an illustration and symbol of national pride, according to which urban
centers transformed into greeneries with plants, flowers and parks. Moreover,
"the greening of the desert [was] always viewed as something positive [...], a
green environment is valued higher than that of the natural, dry desert" (Ouis
2002b: 328). Consequently, the success of "greening the country" was ascribed to
sheikh Zayed. As Ouis (ibid.: 329) quotes from a booklet of sheikh Zayed's private
environmental department, "our country [the UAE] has become a model that has
challenged the hard nature [...]. [It] tells a story of a man's determination to challenge difficult situations and to achieve, what some people call, the impossible"
(Private Department of HH Sheikh Zayed bin Sultan Al Nahyan 1997: 9, quoted
from Ouis 2002b). According to Ouis (2002b: 328), the initiation of greeneries
serves the legitimization of power for the ruling family and the political system of
paternalism. It has been labeled with the term "Zayedism" (Koury 1980: 137f).
Sheikh Zayed's interest in and engagement with the environment is interpreted
as the result of local embeddedness and his Islamic faith.[23] In promotional governmental publications, sheikh Zayed is portrayed as having grown up with the
experience of the harsh desert environment, which taught him that "survival itself was often a major concern" and helped him to develop a knowledge and connection with the country and its wildlife (UAE-US 2020b).

In the context of Masdar City, the Abu Dhabi Sustainability Week and the
"Zayed International Price for the Environment" (see Section 5.3) show that these
beliefs are present and exemplify that connectedness to nature which reflects the
paternalistic image of sheikh Zayed's approach to nature. Masdar officials exploit
this image by describing Masdar City's approach as "a living testament to how

---

23 There is a huge amount of literature on the environment in Islam, see for instance Al-Damkhi
(2008) and Ali (2016). However, not being an expert in this field, I exclude potential assumptions
of Islamic faith that explain the emergence of environmental policy in the UAE. To strengthen
my argument, I quote Ouis (2002b: 324) who states that "in the Emirati environmental discourse,
I find no examples of these particularly eco-theological trends, and none of my informants have
expressed such ideas, other than those found in a general view of Islamic responsibility".

fresh innovative ideas and collaboration can help mold a distinctive and inspiring urban ecosystem" (Masdar 2020b). This is to give the appearance that Masdar City embodies the values and beliefs of the UAE leaders and is symbolic for a national identification with a limited selection of topics in environmental protection.

Furthermore, Ouis (2002b: 338) finds that environmentalism among the UAE population may be "located as an 'imported' discourse", which, however, lacks history, morality and characteristics and motivations of, for example, environmentalist grassroot movements. Instead, environmental topics dominating debates in the UAE society seem adopted from "the global discourse of environmentalism" (ibid.): A brochure of the EFS, for instance, highlights the importance of the "environment's 'balance' with its 'natural cycles'", which is "disturbed [... and] threatened" by humankind (Ouis 2002b: 339).[24] Moreover, the EEG's engagement at the national environment day 2019 underlines the link to global environmental policies, ecological values and beliefs. EGG announced that

> as an accredited body of the UN Environment (UNEP), EEG is proud to announce that the Clean Up UAE campaign will serve as an effective implementation platform for the following sustainable development goals: Goal 11: Sustainable Cities and Communities; Goal 12: Responsible Consumption and Production; 13: Climate Action; Goal 15: Life on Earth; Goal 17: Partnerships for Goals (EEG 2019).

Ouis (2002b: 340) identifies this as a phenomenon of "global concern and a 'same-boat' ideology" to environmental problems. More precisely, it implies a "sav[ing of] the earth" through "global environmental management, kept within its 'carrying capacity' and ecological limits [...], by seeking common environmental policy agreement and through education and information of global citizens" (ibid.). Moreover, according to Macnaghten and Urry (1998: 214), this engagement and societal identification of the "same boat" image results in the citizens' "approval and political support to such programs" and hence increases political legitimacy for the UAE leaders. As a consequence, it leads to a new "rhetoric of partnership and stakeholder democracy", in which the UN, NGOs, governments and businesses cooperate transnationally and achieve a consensus in environmental issues.

---

24 Ouis' (2002b: 339) analysis is based on the journal "Environmental Issues" published by EFS (here: Volume 1, Issue 4, 1996).

6 Conclusions

Built on the foundations of renewable energy production and supply, green and sustainable buildings and architecture, innovation and technology, science and research, institution building, and collaboration with private actors, Masdar City was initiated as part of the Abu Dhabi roadmap 2030, which aims to increase the emirate's economic diversification. Masdar City is a planned city project promoted under the labels of "sustainability" and "ecology". My paper's objective was to link the concept of ecological modernization to aspects of urban sustainability and embed it within the discourse on "smart" cities. First, I explored five "factors" which help to investigate processes of ecological modernization. Based on these factors, I applied the concept of ecological modernization as an analytical tool to investigate which of these factors and to what extent they contribute to the alleged development of ecological modernization in the UAE. Among these factors, various authors have assessed the role of science and technology in preventing environmental hazards. A new generation of innovative technologies is expected to emerge which fulfils the ecological and technological criteria to create cleaner industrial processes. Second, economic pull and push factors are expected to strengthen market dynamics and economic imperatives. More and more, entrepreneurs, innovators, producers, customers, and consumers are regarded as economic agents, who collaborate with public actors in environmental policy. In addition, the concept of ecological modernization presumes a political and institutional change. The traditional "command and control" state is expected to transfer certain assignments to the market and to transform into a participatory, consensual, cooperative and interactive state. Furthermore, the concept of ecological modernization assumes that social groups will become more intensively involved in political decision-making. Activists are expected to act both as a watchdog or partner of political leaders. The concept of ecological modernization expects that the changing interdependence of economy and ecology reflects a change in discursive practices and ideology. Moreover, it expects a stronger focus on and an increased acceptance of technological innovation by economists and ecologists. The spread of environmental knowledge and facts are presumed to shape citizens' ecological consciousness and influence the individuals' environmental behavior.

Certainly, this paper's topic embodies a paradox when one considers the UAE's enormous negative environmental impact while becoming a global leader in renewable energy. In fact, the case of Masdar City has revealed that only two of the formulated factors contribute to the development of ecological modernization in the UAE. Above all, my study proposed that technology and innovation

https://doi.org/10.1515/9783110749298-006

play an important role in the context of Masdar City. In the field of renewable energy, Masdar has invested and developed domestic projects which concentrate on energy production by CSP, PV, wind and waste. Masdar has also engaged in collaborations outside the UAE, which have resulted in projects that are internationally recognized and renowned. The CCUS project represents the core of Masdar's portfolio, which clearly aims to gain economic benefits on the international carbon market. Masdar City was implemented and has been run by a public institution that acts like a private company. However, as it is led by members of the ruling families, it is subject to their political and economic interests and their willingness to provide funding. Moreover, Masdar City established a free trade and investment zone in order to attract international stakeholders. It strengthened its position by winning IRENA's headquarters for Masdar City. Furthermore, with regard to political modernization, certain institutional structures on the federal level as well as on the emirate level of Abu Dhabi were created and implemented for Masdar City. Yet, all environmental decisions are made by the private departments of sheikh Zayed and his successors. Only a few social environmental groups are active in the UAE. However, they have been established and financed by the government, too. Therefore, their work and projects rely on and comply with official UAE politics. The work of these environmental groups has had very little impact on what I analyzed as changing discursive practices and ideology. I only find a vague expression of an "ecological consciousness", that is, an increased interest and knowledge among UAE citizens in ecology and the environment, particularly among young people. Even if ecology and nature represent topics within the societal discourse linked to personal convictions by UAE founding father sheikh Zayed, officials instrumentalize these topics to mark a "good" environmental behavior with notions of national pride and identity.

Consequently, even if technological innovation and economic imperatives appear as relevant push factors for the development of Masdar City, political modernization has only marginally evolved. Social behavior and changing discursive practices and ideology do not have a noticeable impact on the environmental reform processes. More precisely, the absence of democratic participation corresponds to a political atmosphere in which the involvement of the citizens is not considered a prerequisite for environmental reform.[25]

However, the analytical concept of ecological modernization may gain relevance through a "prescriptive policy perspective" (see Frijns et al. 2000: 285).

---

25 This contrasts with the scholarly consensus that democratic structures seem necessary for a preventive and sustainable reduction of environmental impacts (Crot 2013: 2810; see also Dryzek 2000; York et al. 2003).

According to this perspective, ecological modernization in a normative under-standing may offer opportunities to governments for economic transformation and the deepening of state-society relationships that drive ecological progress. The case of Masdar City highlights that new public-private arrangements may shape environmental reform processes and connect public officials to citizens and private organizations. This interwovenness may play an important role for a reciprocal "state-society embeddedness" and might result in designing new mechanisms for the enhancement of environmental policy (ibid.: 286; see also Salau 1997: 277).

Another aspect that plays a role here is the global discourse and the state's reputation or "branding" in the international context. Masdar City was initiated during a period in which global environmental and climate problems have started to be dealt with on a global level. Whereas the Brundtland report in 1987 highlighted the imperative for a global action regarding the "ecological ques-tion", the adoption of the UNFCCC in 1992 set the landmark for binding green-house gas emissions based on scientific consensus and made climate policy an issue of high politics.[26] Therefore, shortly after the UAE's ratification of the Kyoto Protocol in 2005, the 2006 initiation of Masdar City appeared to "follow" the global discourse. Furthermore, I argue that Masdar City has been part of the "self-branding" or "self-image" strategy of the UAE. National "self-images" are con-ceptions of national interests and perceptions of history, both positive and nega-tive, that "are an important dimension of political culture and are transmitted by agents of that culture" and influence a state's behavior in foreign affairs (Kaplo-witz 1990: 47). Clearly, global climate and environmental action present a topic of "good" governance or global "betterment" in today's socio-political context (Henrikson 2005: 75), so that a country carrying out environmental protection measures would contribute to the "global public good" of an intact environment and become internationally recognized and rewarded for its engagement (ibid.: 68).

Without question, this research has been subject to my interpretations of eco-logical modernization and environmental reform in the UAE. Furthermore, my research faced challenges in the collection of official data on the Masdar initia-tive. In this regard, I dealt with limitations in the availability of information on the origins of Masdar City and its political implementation process. Reflections by other researchers and scholars proved helpful in comparing observations and finding discrepancies within information provided by the UAE and Abu Dhabi government and secondary sources. Luomi (2009: 105), for instance, mentions

---

26 As defined by Barnett (1990: 531).

the lack of accessible political historical material and emphasizes that published primary data are not always correct and difficult to interpret. Generally speaking, this reflects what Ahram and Goode (2016: 838) point out as one of the difficulties of studying contemporary authoritarian regimes. Moreover, my research only marginally includes a technical impact assessment with regard to developed technologies and innovation, but rather focused on the policy in the context of environmental reform in the UAE. Nevertheless, my analysis has shown that only the two factors of technological innovation and economic aspects formulated by the concept of ecological modernization are present in the case of Masdar City. Masdar City is shaped by the economic benefits that drive the utopic vision of feasibility in ecological modernization while social impacts and social justice have so far been neglected. Masdar lacks the necessary political modernization to open for a profound structural change and the transformation of environmental reform.

Literature

Abbasi, Tasneem/Premalatha, M./Abbasi, S. A. 2012: Masdar City: A Zero Carbon, Zero Waste Myth, in: Current Science 102/1, 12.

Abgeordnetenhaus von Berlin 1982: Plenarprotokoll 14/9 Berlin.

Abu Dhabi UPC (Abu Dhabi Urban Planning Council) 2016: The Pearl Rating System for Estidama: Public Realm Rating System Design & Construction, Abu Dhabi: UPC.

ADIA (Abu Dhabi Investment Authority) 2020: 2019 Review: Prudent Global Growth, Abu Dhabi: ADIA.

Ahram, Ariel I./Goode, J. Paul 2016: Researching Authoritarianism in the Discipline of Democracy, in: Social Science Quarterly 97/4, 834-849.

Al-Amir, Jawaher/Abu-Hijleh, Bassam 2013: Strategies and Policies from Promoting the Use of Renewable Energy Resource in the UAE, in: Renewable and Sustainable Energy Reviews 26, 660-667.

Al-Damkhi, Ali M. 2008: Environmental Ethics in Islam: Principles, Violations, and Future Perspectives, in: International Journal of Environmental Studies 65/1, 11-31.

Al Qatami, Humaid 1995: The Environment in the UAE: The Present and the Future, in: Al-Hassan, Yousef (ed.): The Dialogue Between Civilizations: The United Arab Emirates and the Federal Republic of Germany, Amman/Sharjah: Friedrich Ebert Foundation and Emirates Centre for Developmental and Strategic Research, 241-254.

Al-Saidi, Mohammad /Elagib, Nadir A. 2018: Ecological Modernization and Responses for a Low-Carbon Future in the Gulf Cooperation Council Countries, in: Wiley Interdisciplinary Reviews: Climate Change 9/4, e528-n/a.

Al-Saidi, Mohammad/Zaidan, Esmat/Hammad, Suzanne 2019: Participation Modes and Diplomacy of Gulf Cooperation Council (GCC) Countries Towards the Global Sustainability Agenda, in: Development in Practice 29/5, 545-558.

Albino, Vito/Berardi, Umberto/Dangelico, Rosa M. 2015: Smart Cities: Definitions, Dimensions, Performance, and Initiatives, in: Journal of Urban Technology 22/1, 3-12.

Ali, Saleem H. 2016: Reconciling Islamic Ethics, Fossil Fuel Dependence, and Climate Change in the Middle East, in: Review of Middle East Studies 50/2, 172-178.

Almheiri, Abdulla K. 2015: Is the United Arab Emirates Capable to Create a Green and Sustainable Future? Unpublished Dissertation, Faculty of Engineering & Information Technology, Dubai: The British University.

Antrobus, Derek 2011: Smart Green Cities: From Modernization to Resilience? In: Urban Research & Practice 4/2, 207-214.

Art, David 2016: Archivists and Adventurers: Research Strategies for Authoritarian Regimes of the Past and Present, in: Social Science Quarterly 97/4, 974-990.

Aspinall, Simon 2001: Environmental Development and Protection in the UAE, in: Al-Abed, Ibrahim (ed.): United Arab Emirates: A New Perspective, London: Trident Publications, 277-304.

Atalay, Yasemin/Biermann, Frank/Kalfagianni, Agni 2016: Adoption of Renewable Energy Technologies in Oil-Rich Countries: Explaining Policy Variation in the Gulf Cooperation Council States, in: Renewable Energy 85, 206-214.

Azadeh, Ali/Fam, Iraj M./Nouri, Jafar/Azadeh, Mansoureh A. 2008: Integrated Health, Safety, Environment and Ergonomics Management System (HSEE-MS): An Efficient Substitution for Conventional HSE-MS, in: Journal of Scientific and Industrial Research 67, 403-411.

https://doi.org/10.1515/9783110749298-007

Badham, Richard 1984: The Sociology of Industrial and Post-Industrial Societies, in: Current Sociology 32/1, 1-141.

Barnett, Michael 1990: High Politics Is Low Politics: The Domestic and Systematic Sources of Israeli Security Policy, 1967-1977, in: World Politics 42/4, 529-562.

Bazoobandi, Sara 2013: The Political Economy of the Gulf Sovereign Wealth Funds: A Case Study of Iran, Kuwait, Saudi Arabia and the United Arab Emirates, Abingdon: Routledge.

Bennett, Andrew/Elman, Colin 2006: Qualitative Research: Recent Developments in Case Study Methods, in: Annual Review of Political Science 9, 455-476.

BioRegional 2017: One Planet Principles, https://www.bioregional.com/resources/one-planet-living-principles (accessed 23 February 2021).

Bloomberg 2019: Capital Markets: Company Overview of Masdar Clean Tech Fund, L.P., https://www.bloomberg.com/research/stocks/private/snapshot.asp?privcapId=32336876 (accessed 11 December 2019; link has expired).

Blowers, Andrew 1997: Environmental Policy: Ecological Modernisation or the Risk Society? In: Urban Studies 34/5-6, 845-871.

Bonnett, Michael 2000: Environmental Concern and the Metaphysics of Education, in: Journal of Philosophy of Education 34/4, 591-602.

Bridge, Sam 2020: UAE's Masdar Signs Deal to Build 200MW Solar Plant in Azerbaijan, in: Arabian Business, 10 January.

Brorman Jensen, Boris 2014: Masdar City: A Critical Retrospection, in: Wippel, Steffen/Bromber, Katrin/Steiner, Christian/Krawietz, Birgit (eds.): Under Construction: Logics of Urbanism in the Gulf Region, Farnham: Ashgate, 45-54.

Bunce, Valerie J./Wolchik, Sharon L. 2010: Defeating Dictators: Electoral Change and Stability in Competitive Authoritarian Regimes, in: World Politics 62/1, 43-86.

Buttel, Frederick H. 2009: Ecological Modernization as Social Theory, in: Mol, Arthur P. J./Sonnenfeld, David A./Spaargaren, Gert (eds.): The Ecological Modernisation Reader: Environmental Reform in Theory and Practice, New York, NY/London: Routledge, 123-140.

Choy, Er Ah 2007: A Quantitative Methodology to Test Ecological Modernization Theory in the Malaysian Context, PhD Thesis, Wageningen: Wageningen University.

Cohen, Maurie J. 2000: Ecological Modernisation, Environmental Knowledge and National Character: A Preliminary Analysis of the Netherlands, in: Environmental Politics 9/1, 77-106.

Crot, Laurence 2013: Planning for Sustainability in Non-democratic Polities: The Case of Masdar City, in: Urban Studies 50/13, 2809-2825.

Cugurullo, Federico 2013a: How to Build a Sandcastle: An Analysis of the Genesis and Development of Masdar City, in: Journal of Urban Technology 20/1, 23-37.

Cugurullo, Federico 2013b: The Business of Utopia: Estidama and the Road to the Sustainable City, in: Utopian Studies 24/1, 66-88.

Cugurullo, Federico 2016a: Speed Kills: Fast Urbanism and Endangered Sustainability in the Masdar City Project, in: Datta, Ayona/Shaban, Abdul (eds.): Mega-Urbanization in the Global South: Fast Cities and New Urban Utopias of the Postcolonial State, London: Routledge.

Cugurullo, Federico 2016b: Urban Eco-Modernisation and the Policy Context of New Eco-City Projects: Where Masdar City Fails and Why, in: Urban Studies 53/11, 2417-2433.

Dargin, Justin 2010: Addressing the UAE Natural Gas Crisis: Strategies for a Rational Energy Policy, Harvard Kennedy School Dubai Initiative, Cambridge, MA: Belfer Center for Science and International Affairs.

Davoudi, Simin/Crawford, Jenny/Mehmood, Abid 2009: Climate Change and Spatial Planning Responses, in: Davoudi, Simin/Crawford, Jenny/Mehmood, Abid (eds.): Planning for Climate Change: Strategies for Mitigation and Adaptation for Spatial Planners, London: Routledge, 7-18.

De Jong, Martin/Joss, Simon/Schraven, Daan /Zhan, Changjie/Weijnen, Margot 2015: Sustainable - Smart - Resilient - Low Carbon - Eco - Knowledge Cities: Making Sense of a Multitude of Concepts Promoting Sustainable Urbanization, in: Journal of Cleaner Production 109, 25-38.

Doukas, Haris/Patlitzianas, Konstantinos D./Kagiannas, Argyris G./Psarras, John 2006: Renewable Energy Sources and Rationale Use of Energy Development in the Dountries of GCC: Myth or Reality? In: Renewable Energy 31/6, 755-770.

Doulet, Jean-François 2016: Retour à Masdar City: Un urbanisme au prisme de l'émergence, in: Texier, Simon/Doulet, Jean-François (eds.): Abou Dhabi: Stade ultime du modernisme, Paris: Éditions B2, 111-165.

Dryzek, John S. 2000: Deliberative Democracy and Beyond: Liberals, Critics, Contestations, Oxford: Oxford University Press.

EAD (Environment Agency Abu Dhabi) 2017: Abu Dhabi State of Environment Report 2017, Abu Dhabi: EAD.

EEG (Emirates Environmental Group) 2019: EEG Celebrates National Environment Day, https://www.eeg-uae.org/eeg-celebrates-national-environment-day/ (accessed 17 March 2020).

EEG (Emirates Environmental Group) 2020a: About EEG, https://www.eeg-uae.org/about-eeg/ (accessed 14 February 2020).

EEG (Emirates Environmental Group) 2020b: Educational Programmes, https://www.eeg-uae.org/educational-programme/ (accessed 21 February 2020).

EIA (US Energy Information Administration) 2017: Country Analysis Brief: United Arab Emirates, Policy Brief, Washington, DC: EIA.

El-Kharouf, Farouk/Al-Qudsi, Sulayman/Obeid, Shifa 2010: The Gulf Corporation Council Sovereign Wealth Funds: Are They Instruments for Economic Diversification or Political Tools? In: Asian Economic Papers 9/1, 124-151.

Emirates Nature-WWF 2018: Emirates Nature-WWF Strategy 2015-2020, Abu Dhabi: Emirates Nature-WWF.

Emirates Nature-WWF 2019: Survey Finds UAE Youth Want To Protect Our Environment and Take Part In More Nature Based Activities & Events, Abu Dhabi: Emirates Nature-WWF.

EU 2019: Fossil CO_2 and GHG Emissions of All World Countries: 2019 Report, Luxembourg: EU.

Fichter, Donn 1964: Individualized Automatic Transit and the City, Providence, RI: B.H. Sikes.

Foreman, Colin 2007: City of the Future: The Carbon-Neutral City Being Built in the Abu Dhabi Desert under the Masdar Initiative Could Set a Standard for Sustainable Development Across the Region and Beyond, Special Report: Alternative Energy, in: MEED Middle East Economic Digest 51/32, 25.

Freedom House 2020: Freedom In The World 2019: United Arab Emirates, https://freedomhouse.org/country/united-arab-emirates/freedom-world/2019 (accessed 16 April 2020).

Frijns, Jos/Phuong, Phung Thuy/Mol, Arthur P. J. 2000: Ecological Modernisation Theory and Industrialising Economies: The Case of Viet Nam, in: Environmental Politics 9/1, 257-292.

Gallup 2011: The United Arab Emirates at 40: A Success Story, https://news.gallup.com/poll/157061/united-arab-emirates-success-story.aspx (accessed 23 February 2021).

Gallup 2020: Publications United Arab Emirates, https://news.gallup.com/topic/country_
   are.aspx (accessed 20 February 2020).
Gerring, John 2004: What Is a Case Study and What Is It Good for? In: The American Political
   Science Review 98/2, 341-354.
Gilley, Bruce 2012: Authoritarian Environmentalism and China's Response to Climate Change,
   in: Environmental Politics 21/2, 287-307.
Goldsmith, Edward/Allen, Robert 1972: A Blueprint for Survival, in: The Ecologist 2/1, 1-43.
Günel, Gökçe 2019: Spaceship in the Desert: Energy, Climate Change, and Urban Design in Abu
   Dhabi, Durham: Duke University Press.
Hajer, Maarten A. 1995: The Politics of Environmental Discourse: Ecological Modernization and
   the Policy Process, Oxford: Oxford University Press.
Haouas, Ilham/Heshmati, Almas 2014: Can the UAE Avoid the Oil Curse by Economic Diversifi-
   cation? IZA Discussion Papers No. 8003, Bonn: Institute of Labor Economics.
Hartje, Volkmar J. 1990: Zur Struktur des "ökologisierten" Kapitalstocks: Variablen und Deter-
   minanten umweltsparender technologischer Anpassungen in Unternehmen, in: Zimmer-
   mann, Klaus W./Hartje, Volkmar J./Ryll, Andreas (eds.): Ökologische Modernisierung der
   Produktion: Strukturen und Trends, Berlin: Edition Sigma, 135-198.
Harvey, David 1989: From Managerialism to Entrepreneurialism: The Transformation in Urban
   Governance in Late Capitalism, in: Geografiska Annaler, Series B, Human Geography 71/1,
   3-17.
Heard-Bey, Frauke 1982: From Trucial States to United Arab Emirates: A Society in Transition,
   London: Longman.
Henrikson, Alan K. 2005: Niche Diplomacy in the World Public Arena: The Global "Corners" of
   Canada and Norway, in: Melissen, Jan (ed.): The New Public Diplomacy: Soft Power in In-
   ternational Relations, London: Palgrave Macmillan UK, 67-87.
Hindley, Angus 2007: Abu Dhabi's New Direction: The Emirate's Masdar Initiative is Looking to
   Bring Solar and Hydrogen Power Generation to the Gulf, Special Report: Masdar: Alterna-
   tive Energy Program, in: MEED Middle East Economic Digest 51/10, 45.
Hollands, Robert G. 2008: Will the Real Smart City Please Stand up? In: City 12/3, 303-320.
Huber, Joseph 1983: Humanökologie als Grundlage einer präventiven Umweltpolitik? Berlin:
   Internationales Institut für Umwelt und Gesellschaft, Wissenschaftszentrum Berlin.
Huber, Joseph 1985: Die Regenbogen-Gesellschaft: Ökologie und Sozialpolitik, Frankfurt am
   Main: Fischer.
Huber, Joseph 1989: Technikbilder: Weltanschauliche Weichenstellungen der Technologie- und
   Umweltpolitik, Wiesbaden: VS Verlag für Sozialwissenschaften.
Huber, Joseph 1993: Ökologische Modernisierung: Zwischen bürokratischem und zivilgesell-
   schaftlichem Handeln, in: von Prittwitz, Volker (ed.): Umweltpolitik als Modernisierungs-
   prozess: Politikwissenschaftliche Umweltforschung und -lehre in der Bundesrepublik
   Deutschland, Opladen: Leske + Budrich, 51-69.
Huber, Joseph 1995: Nachhaltige Entwicklung: Strategien für eine ökologische und soziale Erd-
   politik, Berlin: Edition Sigma.
Huber, Joseph 2004: New Technologies and Environmental Innovation, Cheltenham: Edward
   Elgar.
Hvidt, Martin 2013: Economic Diversification in GCC Countries: Past Record and Future Trends,
   Kuwait Programme on Development, Governance and Globalisation in the Gulf States, LSE
   Paper No. 27, London: London School of Economics and Political Science.

IRENA (International Renewable Energy Agency) 2019: Renewable Energy Market Analysis: GCC 2019, Abu Dhabi: IRENA.

Jänicke, Martin 1993: Ökologische und politische Modernisierung in entwickelten Industriegesellschaften, in: von Prittwitz, Volker (ed.): Umweltpolitik als Modernisierungsprozess: Politikwissenschaftliche Umweltforschung und -lehre in der Bundesrepublik, Opladen: Leske + Budrich, 15-29.

Jänicke, Martin 1996: Erfolgsbedingungen von Umweltpolitik, in: Jänicke, Martin (ed.): Umweltpolitik der Industrieländer: Entwicklung - Bilanz - Erfolgsbedingungen, Berlin: Edition Sigma, 9-28.

Jones, Russel 2008: Masdar Initiative in Abu Dhabi Focuses on Alternative Energy Sources, in: Civil Engineering: Magazine of the South African Institution of Civil Engineering 16/8, 64.

Jörgens, Helge 1996: Die Institutionalisierung von Umweltpolitik im internationalen Vergleich, in: Jänicke, Martin (ed.): Umweltpolitik der Industrieländer: Entwicklung - Bilanz - Erfolgsbedingungen, Berlin: Edition Sigma, 59-112.

Kaplowitz, Noel 1990: National Self-Images, Perception of Enemies, and Conflict Strategies: Psychopolitical Dimensions of International Relations, in: Political Psychology 11/1, 39-82.

Kazerouni, Alexandre 2017: Le Miroir des Cheikhs: Musée et politique dans les principautés du golfe Persique, Paris: Presses Universitaires de France.

Khodr, Hiba/Reiche, Danyel 2012: The Specialized Cities of the Gulf Cooperation Council: A Case Study of a Distinct Type of PolicyInnovation and Diffusion, in: Digest of Middle East Studies 21/1, 149-177.

Kitschelt, Herbert 1983: Politik und Energie: Energie-Technologiepolitiken in den USA, der Bundesrepublik Deutschland, Frankreich und Schweden, Frankfurt am Main/New York, NY: Campus.

Koury, Enver M. 1980: The United Arab Emirates: Its Political System and Politics, Hyattsville, MD: Institute of Middle Eastern and North African Affairs.

Kowalski, Przemyslaw/Büge, Max/Sztajerowska, Monika/Egeland, Matias 2013: State-Owned Enterprises: Trade Effects and Policy Implications, OECD Trade Policy Papers No. 147, Paris: OECD Publishing.

KU (Khalifa University) 2018: Masdar Institute, https://www.ku.ac.ae/institute/masdar-institute/ (accessed 18 January 2020).

Lélé, Sharachchandra M. 1991: Sustainable Development: A Critical Review, in: World Development 19/6, 607-621.

Low, Linda 2012: Abu Dhabi's Vision 2030: An Ongoing Journey of Economic Development, Singapore: World Scientific Publishing.

Luciani, Giacomo 2016: Middle East: Clean Energy Sources and the Diversification of the Oil Economies? In: Revue Internationale et Stratégique 104/4, 143-152.

Luomi, Mari 2009: Abu Dhabi's Alternative-Energy Initiatives: Seizing Climate-Change Opportunities, in: Middle East Policy 16/4, 102-117.

Luomi, Mari 2014: Mainstreaming Climate Policy in the Gulf Cooperation Council States, OIES Working Paper MEP 7, Oxford: The Oxford Institute for Energy Studies.

Macnaghten, Phil/Urry, John 1998: Contested Natures, London: Sage.

MADFEC (Masdar Abu Dhabi Future Energy Company) 2009: Today's Source for Tomorrow's Energy, Abu Dhabi: MADFEC.

Madichie, Nnamdi O. 2011: IRENA - Masdar City (UAE) - Exemplars of Innovation into Emerging Markets, in: foresight 13/6, 34-47.

Mascarenhas, Prianjali 2018: The Transfer and Mobilisation of Sustainability Concepts to Abu
    Dhabi: The Case of Masdar and the Urban Planning Council, PhD Thesis, The Department
    of Geography and Environment, London: The London School of Economics and Political
    Science.
Masdar 2010: Why is Masdar City Sustainable? Abu Dhabi: Masdar.
Masdar 2012: Sustainability Report 2012, https://masdar.ae/en/about-us/useful-links/an-
    nual-and-industry-reports (accessed 24 February 2021).
Masdar 2016a: MENA's First Carbon Capture Utilisation & Storage (CCUS) Project Now on
    Stream, https://news.masdar.ae/en/news/2018/11/28/09/55/menas-first-carbon-cap-
    ture-utilisation--amp-storage-ccus-project-now-on-stream-23 (accessed 18 January 2020).
Masdar 2016b: Sustainability Report 2016, https://masdar.ae/en/about-us/useful-links/an-
    nual-and-industry-reports (accessed 24 February 2021).
Masdar 2017: Masdar City: The Source of Innovation and Sustainability, https://masdar.ae/
    en/masdar-city/plan-yourvisit/explore-the-city (accessed 24 February 2021).
Masdar 2018b: Sustainability Report 2018, https://masdar.ae/en/about-us/useful-links/an-
    nual-and-industry-reports (accessed 24 February 2021).
Masdar 2019a: Masdar City Eco-Villa Net Zero Energy Flyer, https://masdar.ae/en/masdar-
    city/the-city/sustainability (accessed 24 February 2021).
Masdar 2019c: Masdar Clean Energy Fact Sheet, https://masdar.ae/en/new-news-and-events/
    media (accessed 24 February 2021).
Masdar 2020a: Masdar Clean Energy Projects, https://masdar.ae/en/masdar-clean-energy/
    projects (accessed 16 January 2020).
Masdar 2020b: Masdar City Fact Sheet, https://masdar.ae/en/new-news-and-events/media
    (accessed 24 February 2021).
Masdar 2020d: Masdar Free Zone, https://masdar.ae/en/new-news-and-events/media (ac-
    cessed 24 February 2021).
Masdar 2020e: Abu Dhabi Sustainability Week (ADSW), https://masdar.ae/en/strategic-plat-
    forms/adsw (accessed 9 February 2020).
Masdar 2020f: Annual and Industry Reports, https://masdar.ae/en/about-us/useful-links/an-
    nual-and-industry-reports (accessed 16 February 2020).
Masdar 2020g: Masdar Achieves Financial Close on Landmark 100 MW Nur Navoi Solar Project
    in Uzbekistan, https://news.masdar.ae/en/news/2020/12/23/08/20/masdar-achieves-
    financial-close-on-landmark-100-mw-nur-navoi-solar-project-in-uzbekistan (accessed
    3 January 2021).
Masdar 2020h: Masdar and Uzbekistan Government to Develop Landmark 500MW Wind Pro-
    ject, https://news.masdar.ae/en/news/2020/06/09/11/47/masdar-and-uzbekistan-gov-
    ernment-to-develop-landmark-500mw-wind-project (accessed 3 January 2021).
Masdar Free Zone 2020: Masdar City to Host the "Green Run" with the UAE's Environment
    Friends Society, https://masdarcityfreezone.com/en/news/masdar-city-to-host-the-
    green-run-with-the-uaes-environment-friends-society (accessed 14 February 2020).
MOCCAE (UAE Ministry of Climate Change and Environment) 2017: National Environment Day,
    https://www.moccae.gov.ae/en/knowledge-and-statistics/national-environment-
    day.aspx (accessed 10 February 2020).
MOCCAE (UAE Ministry of Climate Change and Environment) 2018: About the Ministry,
    https://www.moccae.gov.ae/en/about-ministry/about-the-ministry.aspx (accessed 10
    February 2020).

Mol, Arthur P. J. 1995: The Refinement of Production: Ecological Modernization Theory and the Chemical Industry, Utrecht: Van Arkel.

Mol, Arthur P. J. 1997: Ecological Modernization: Industrial Transformations and Environmental Reform, in: Redclift, Michael R./Woodgate, Graham (eds.): The International Handbook of Environmental Sociology, Cheltenham: Elgar, 138-149.

Mol, Arthur P. J. 2000: The Environmental Movement in an Era of Ecological Modernisation, in: Geoforum 31/1, 45-56.

Mol, Arthur P. J. 2001: Globalization and Environmental Reform: The Ecological Modernization of the Global Economy, Cambridge, MA: The MIT Press.

Mol, Arthur P. J. 2002: Ecological Modernization and the Global Economy, in: Global Environmental Politics 2/2, 92-115.

Mol, Arthur P. J./Sonnenfeld, David A. 2000: Ecological Modernisation Around the World: An Introduction, in: Environmental Politics 9/1, 1-14.

Mol, Arthur P. J./Spaargaren, Gert 1992: Sociology, Environment, and Modernity: Ecological Modernization as a Theory of Social Change, in: Society and Natural Resources 5/4, 323-344.

Mol, Arthur P. J./Spaargaren, Gert/Sonnenfeld, David A. 2009: Ecological Modernisation: Three Decades of Policy, Practice and Theoretical Reflection, in: Mol, Arthur P. J./Sonnenfeld, David A./Spaargaren, Gert (eds.): The Ecological Modernisation Reader: Environmental Reform in Theory and Practice, New York, NY and London: Routledge, 3-14.

Mubadala 2020a: Who We Are, https://www.mubadala.com/en/who-we-are/about-the-company (accessed 10 February 2020).

Mubadala 2020b: 2019: Annual Review, https://www.mubadala.com/annual-review-2019/index.php (accessed 24 February 2021).

Mubadala Petroleum 2017: Operating Responsibly Report 2017, http://www.mubadalapetroleum.com/docs/default-source/publications/mp-csr-report-2017.pdf?sfvrsn=2 (accessed 24 February 2021).

Mueller, Katharina/Sgouridis, Sgouris P. 2011: Simulation-Based Analysis of Personal Rapid Transit Systems: Service and Energy Performance Assessment of the Masdar City PRT Case, in: Journal of Advanced Transportation, Special Issue: Modeling and Optimization of Transportation Systems 45/4, 252-270.

Nader, Sam 2009: Paths to a Low-Carbon Economy: The Masdar Example, in: Energy Procedia 1/1, 3951-3958.

Naím, Moisés 2009: What Is A Gongo? In: Mansbach, Richard W. (ed.): Global Politics in a Changing World: A Reader, Belmont, CA: Wadsworth, 222-224.

One Planet Network 2020a: Global SCP Projects Database, https://www.oneplanetnetwork.org/initiatives#block-search-form--2 (accessed 20 February 2020).

One Planet Network 2020b: Global SCP Projects Database: United Arab Emirates, https://www.oneplanetnetwork.org/initiatives?f%5B0%5D=sm_field_countries%3Ataxonomy_term%3A247#block-search-form--2 (accessed 16 February 2020).

Ouis, Pernilla 2002a: "Greening the Emirates": The Modern Construction of Nature in the United Arab Emirates, in: Cultural Geographies 9, 334-347.

Ouis, Pernilla 2002b: Power, Person, and Place: Tradition, Modernity, and Environment in the United Arab Emirates, Human Ecology Division, PhD Thesis, Lund: Lund University.

Ouis, Pernilla 2010: "And an Island Never Cries": Cultural and Societal Perspectives on the Mega Development of Islands in the United Arab Emirates, in: Badescu, Viorel/Cathcart, Richard (eds.): Macro-Engineering Seawater in Unique Environments, Berlin and Heidelberg: Springer, 59-75.

Ouis, Pernilla 2011: Engineering the Emirates: The Evolution of a New Environment, in: Brunn, Stanley D. (ed.): Engineering Earth: The Impacts of Mega-Engineering Projects, New York, NY: Springer, 1409-1423.

Owens, Susan 1994: Land, Limits and Sustainability: A Conceptual Framework and Some Dilemmas for the Planning System, in: Transactions of the Institute of British Geographers 19/4, 439-456.

Private Department of HH Sheikh Zayed bin Sultan Al Nahyan 1997: [Booklet about Sheikh Zayed's Work for the Environment in the UAE], Abu Dhabi: Private Department of HH Sheikh Zayed bin Sultan Al Nahyan.

Raouf, Mohammed 2008: Climate Change Threats, Opportunities, and the GCC Countries, Middle East Institute Policy Brief No. 12, Washington, DC: Middle East Institute.

Reiche, Danyel 2010a: Energy Policies of Gulf Cooperation Council (GCC) Countries: Possibilities and Limitations of Ecological Modernization in Rentier States in: Energy Policy 38/5, 2395-2403.

Reiche, Danyel 2010b: Renewable Energy Policies in the Gulf Countries: A Case Study of the Carbon-Neutral "Masdar City" in Abu Dhabi, in: Energy Policy 38/1, 378-382.

Reiche, Danyel 2010c: Sovereign Wealth Funds as a New Instrument of Climate Protection Policy? A Case Study of Norway as a Pioneer of Ethical Guidelines for Investment Policy, in: Energy 35, 3569-3577.

Richardson, Benjamin 2011: Sovereign Wealth Funds and the Quest for Sustainability: Insights from Norway and New Zealand, in: Nordic Journal of Commercial Law 2, 1-27.

Routledge Encyclopedia (Routledge Encyclopedia of International Political Economy) 2001: Diversification, Volume 1, Entries A-F, London: Routledge, 360-361.

Rozanov, Andrew 2005: Who Holds the Wealth of Nations? In: Central Banking Journal 15/4, 52-57.

Rugh, William 1997: The United Arab Emirates: What Are the Sources of its Stability? In: Middle East Policy 5/3, 14-24.

Salau, Fatai K. 1997: Nigeria, in: Jänicke, Martin/Weidner, Helmut (eds.): National Environmental Policies: A Comparative Study of Capacity-Building, Berlin: Springer, 257-278.

SCAD (Statistics Centre Abu Dhabi) 2018: Statistical Yearbook of Abu Dhabi 2018, https://www.scad.gov.abudhabi/Release%20Documents/SYB_2018_EN_9Sep.pdf (accessed 24 February 2021).

Schnaiberg, Allan 1980: The Environment: From Surplus to Scarcity, New York, NY: Oxford University Press.

Shayah, M. Hazem 2015: Economic Diversification by Boosting Non-Oil Exports (Case of UAE) in: Journal of Economics, Business and Management 3/7, 735-738.

Sun, Xiaolei/Li, Jianping/Wang, Yongfeng/Clark, Woodrow W. 2014: China's Sovereign Wealth Fund Investments in Overseas Energy: The Energy Security Perspective, in: Energy Policy 65, 654-661.

SWFI (Sovereign Wealth Fund Institute) 2020a: What is a Sovereign Wealth Fund? https://www.swfinstitute.org/research/sovereign-wealth-fund (accessed 30 January 2020).

SWFI (Sovereign Wealth Fund Institute) 2020b: Top 88 Largest Sovereign Wealth Fund Rankings by Total Assets, https://www.swfinstitute.org/fund-rankings/sovereign-wealth-fund (accessed 30 January 2020).

Taryam, Abdullah O. 1987: The Establishment of the United Arab Emirates 1950-85, London: Croom Helm.

Texier, Simon/Doulet, Jean-François 2016: Abou Dhabi: Stade ultime du modernisme, Paris: Éditions B2.

Thacker, Sunil/SK, George 2021: Environmental Law and Practice in the United Arab Emirates: Overview, https://uk.practicallaw.thomsonreuters.com/w-008-3980?originationContext=document&transitionType=DocumentItem&contextData=(sc.Default)&firstPage=true (accessed 5 February 2021).

The Abu Dhabi Executive Council 2007: Policy Agenda 2007-2008: The Emirate of Abu Dhabi, Abu Dhabi: The Abu Dhabi Executive Council.

The Government of Abu Dhabi 2008: The Abu Dhabi Economic Vision 2030, Abu Dhabi: The Government of Abu Dhabi.

The World Bank 2006: Held by the Visible Hand: The Challenge of State-Owned Enterprise Corporate Governance for Emerging Markets, Washington, DC: The World Bank.

The World Bank 2020: World Development Indicators: Long Definition and Methodology, Washington, DC: The World Bank.

Theeyattuparampil, Vijo/Auktor, Georgeta/Alsaleh, Yasser 2013: Challenges and Opportunities for the Emerging Carbon Capture, Utilisation and Storage Innovation System in the United Arab Emirates, in: International Journal of Innovation and Learning 13/3, 284-307.

Theys, Jacques 2011: Les villes "post-carbone" moteurs de l'économie verte de demain? In: Annales des Mines: Responsabilité et Environnement 61, 128-133.

UAE-US (The Embassy of the UAE to the US) 2020a: Masdar Initiative Supports Clean Energy, News and Media Report, https://www.uae-embassy.org/news-media/masdar-initiative-supports-clean-energy (accessed 27 February 2020).

UAE-US (The Embassy of the UAE to the US) 2020b: Sheikh Zayed bin Sultan Al Nahyan, Founder of the UAE, https://www.uae-embassy.org/about-uae/history/sheikh-zayed-bin-sultan-al-nahyan-founder-uae (accessed 21 February 2020).

UAE Government (The Government of the United Arab Emirates) 2019: Waste-To-Energy, https://u.ae/en/information-and-services/environment-and-energy/water-and-energy/types-of-energy-sources/waste-to-energy- (accessed 3 June 2021).

Ulrichsen, Kristian C. 2017: The United Arab Emirates: Power, Politics and Policy-Making, Abingdon: Routledge.

UNCTAD (United Nations Conference on Trade and Development) 2019: World Investment Report 2019: Country Fact Sheet United Arab Emirates, New York, NY: UNCTAD.

UNFCCC (United Nations Framework Convention on Climate Change) 2016: The Concept of Economic Diversification in the Context of Response Measures: Technical Paper by the Secretariat, New York, NY: UNFCCC.

US EPA (United States Environmental Protection Agency) 2016: Green Building, https://archive.epa.gov/greenbuilding/web/html/about.html (accessed 17 January 2020; link has expired).

van Koppen, Kris/Mol, Arthur P. J. 2009: Ecological Modernisation of Industrial Systems, in: Mol, Arthur P. J./Sonnenfeld, David A./Spaargaren, Gert (eds.): The Ecological Modernisation Reader: Environmental Reform in Theory and Practice, New York, NY/London: Routledge, 295-317.

WCED (World Commission on Environment and Development) 1987: Our Common Future, Oxford: Oxford University Press.

WFES (World Future Energy Summit) 2008: Inaugural Speech of Crown Prince of Abu Dhabi, Sheikh Mohammed bin Zayed al-Nahayan, at the Abu Dhabi National Exhibition Centre on 21 January, Abu Dhabi: WFES.

Woessner, Raymon 2016: Dubaï et Abou Dhabi: La naissance d'un emporium, in: Revue d'Économie Régionale et Urbaine 2016/1, 155-174.

WWF (World Wide Fund For Nature) 2018: Living Planet Report - 2018: Aiming Higher, https://www.wwf.eu/campaigns/living_planet_report_2018/ (acccessed 24 February 2021).

WWF (World Wide Fund For Nature) 2019a: WWF: Conservation Projects, https://wwf.panda.org/knowledge_hub/where_we_work/project/ (accessed 11 February 2020).

WWF (World Wide Fund For Nature) 2019b: WWF Offices: United Arab Emirates, https://wwf.panda.org/wwf_offices/united_arab_emirates/ (accessed 11 February 2020).

York, Richard/Rosa, Eugene A./Dietz, Thomas 2003: Footprints on the Earth: The Environmental Consequences of Modernity, in: American Sociological Review 68/2, 279-300.

Zayed International (Foundation for the Environment) 2020: Zayed International Prize, https://www.zayedprize.org.ae/# (accessed 9 February 2020).

www.ingramcontent.com/pod-product-compliance
Lightning Source LLC
Chambersburg PA
CBHW030853270326

41928CB00008B/1361